WINNER OF THE REGAL AWARD IN
LITERATURE

CHITLINS

**Creative, Helpful, Intuitive, Thoughts,
Lifting, Individuals, Naturally, Seeking**

*Blackshear –
Beautiful, loving, ascending, Compassionate
Kindred, sincere, honorable, elegant*

Keith "Preacher" Brown

angelic, resourceful !!

*Thanks,
Keith
2003*

PUBLISHED BY REGAL PUBLISHING, INC.
2 Burbank Blvd, Savannah, Georgia 31419

CHITLINS

ISBN 0-9717355-0-6

Acknowledgements

First and foremost, I thank God for the gift of life through mercy and grace as well as the gift of writing and motivating the masses. To my loving fiancé Wakea (Nikki), thank you for sacrificing time, rest and other endeavors to type this manuscript. To my son Keon, thanks for saying "Daddy you are Keith preacher Brown, The Motivator of the Millennium-write CHITLINS." To Meleya Saxton and Dr. Josephine Booth (Savannah State University), thanks for your time and typing assistance. To "Team Keith Preacher Brown,"(Theodore and Betty Richardson, Savannah office, Charles and Lily Jones, Stone Mountain/Atlanta office, Anthony Irwin, business manager-deceased-Jackie Mells, accountant Marjerie Roberts, accountant-Tamara Linley, financial consultant - Jenaro Roberts, Complete Source Housing Bureau, Delores Billups-sales, Jurrell Howell, Exec. Asst. - Tykeisha Jordan, consultant-Donald Dupont, Videographer-Daryl Reynolds, photographer-James Scott, computer specialist - Sonji Reddings - Exec. Asst.-Furman Gatewood Jr., Workshop facilitator, Denacio Richardson- Fitness consultant, Sabrina Richardson, Davida Roberts and Jo Carswell –typists for initial CHITLINS idea-and all of you who referred and/or booked "TKPB")-thanks for your sincere loyalty and belief in the vision of uplift and CHITLINS. To TRIO programs, Eastside Players, Dare-2-Care of Claxton and The Sickle Cell Foundation, thanks for being the pinnacle of Generation Excellent…To Savannah State University-Thanks for your continuous nurturing…You can "get anywhere from here…" To the English and Multicultural affairs departments of Georgia Southern University-Thanks for your support and publishing "Mother-More." To Sparrowgrass Poetry Forum Inc. –Thanks for publishing "Young Souls Held at Bay." To Regal Publishing-Thanks for believing in my vision! The best is yet to come. To Shirley Matthews(big sis), Maxine Lewis and Steve Harvey (Frat)- Thanks for the Apollo moments. To Dublin/Laurens County Ga.- Thanks for the uplift and love from 1994-1999. To Bethel A.M.E.(Savannah), St. Paul A.M.E. (Dublin) Springfield Gardens U.M.C(Queens, New York),Elm Grove Baptist(Meridian), and First Evergreen Missionary Baptist(Savannah), thanks for some form of spiritual enhancement. To Fraternal, Professional, Civic organizations (members in the struggle to emancipate youth and each other), teachers, professors, colleagues, students, friends and associates all over the nation, especially in New York and Georgia- THANK YOU for being blessings in my life- You are too numerous to name! Thanks Steve (Leval) for saving my life in '95.

Last but certainly not least, to my Family members- the ones who know my strengths and weaknesses, THANK YOU for all of the little things through the years…God is now turning them into bigger things. I salute you with "Preacher's People."

For some reason, God made you all my people.
For some reason, you all have nurtured me in your own way!
For some reason, I cry out for all of you and these tears travel up to the Creator and say,
"Lord please protect my family."
For some reason, I've always wanted you to love one another.

For some reason, your love and encouragement have made
me ready to soar and make this family proud
(if God spares my life).
For some reason, I want all of us to unite.
For some reason, I want this generation to excel beyond the
last one so that the next one will have an example to follow!
For some reason, a different one of you crosses my mind
each day.
For some reason, God made you all people.

Family
Origin all that I am
Relatives who love in unique ways

Spiritual are my people as they live
Omnipotent is my God, warmth to my people he did give
Moments with each of you that made me laugh and cry
Experiences I'll never forget even after I die.

Remembering the gatherings in different cities and towns.
Especially when we built each other up, not tore each other down.
Always keeping in my heart our family members who are deceased
Saying prayers to God so that we may all have PEACE.
Original are my people filled with bountiful love
Natural are my people, definitely sent from above.

For these reasons: I Love You All!

To all of my nephews, nieces, and little cousins, ask God to
show you your gift and when He does, you had better unwrap it
with enthusiasm! Uncle Keith loves you unconditionally!

Contents

Introduction: *8*

Chapter: 1   Lemon People   10
Chapter: 2   Fragile – Handle with Hair   13
                 "BIONIC" (Skit)   15
Chapter: 3   BIONIC   18
Chapter: 4   Hide and Seek   25
Chapter: 5   Super-vision not Supervision   27
Chapter: 6   Equally Yolked – Not Rotten Eggs 30
Chapter: 7   7 Sensational Days   34
                 "Quotable Quotes"   36
Chapter: 8   Choices vs Voices   37
Chapter: 9   Miracles not Miracle Whip   41
Chapter: 10   Not by Sperm – By Spirit   46
                 "Mother More" (Poem)   53
Chapter: 11   Emancipated by God   55
                 "First AID Kit" (Poem)   58
                 "(Kinder)garten" (Poem)   60
Chapter: 12   Retire or Re-tire   62
Chapter: 13   If it Runs in the Family...   69
Chapter: 14   Tongue Twister   74
Chapter: 15   Spare the rod, Spoil the nation   79
                 "King of the Cast" (Poem)   83
                 "From the Womb to the tomb"   84
Chapter: 16   Dream Walking   86
                 "Young Souls Held at Bay"   89
Chapter: 17   Exalt the Elders   91
Chapter: 18   Haiku Hype   96

"And on the 8th Day" (Poem)   103

Chapter: 19   And on the 8th Day   105

DAP (Poem)   111

Chapter: 20   DAP   113

Chapter: 21   Poetic Praise   116

Chapter: 22   Clearance Sale   126

"America Will Rise Again" (Poem)   130

Chapter: 23   Reflect, Protect and Connect... 132

Introduction

In this world of chaos and hostility -
You must use your God given abilities –
To illustrate that you are an asset, not a liability –
Don't be afraid to practice humility –
Always uplift others, for it is your responsibility –
Then and only then will God provide ultimate stability!

It is not our mission to see through each other; it is our mission to see each other through.

If this were a utopia, we would live to love, support and cherish all those whom we come in contact with. Believe it or not, everyone you converse with, whether casually or formally, whether once a year or daily, whether a stranger, close friend, or relative – has a profound impact on the progression or regression of your life. CHITLINS is a wealth of emotions that have evolved out of the depths of my soul like the lava that overflows profusely out of a volcano. Each poem, quote, or essay will cause a catharsis (purging of emotions) in your life. After reading, re – reading, and examining this work, the person you are will come face-to-face, heart to heart, and soul-to-soul with the person you are destined to become. After that, you will never be able to suppress the gift God placed in you.

Now say the following as if you have just won the five million dollar Publisher's Clearing House jackpot:

I AM SOMEBODY
I WON'T HANG MY HEAD FOR ANYBODY
I'LL UPLIFT EVERYBODY
I AM SOMEBODY and GOD IS ALL!!!

Fasten your literary seatbelts! CHITLINS is prepared to move you into a new realm of action.

1
Lemon People

It is not our mission to see through each other; it is our mission to see each other through.

If you are seeking to grow spiritually, economically, culturally, socially, or intellectually, stay away from negative people. Pray for them but don't stay for them. Negative people will kill your spirit. You can be in their environment but not of their environment. Negative people are easy to spot. They complain eight hours a day, sulk, plot, and point fingers for eight hours, and sleep for the other eight. Realistically, we are all negative at some point during the season, but there are some people who inflict frostbite on our dreams during the summertime of our lives. These are the people who you avoid in the malls, grocery stores, churches, and in the workplace. Some of them even fester in our homes. Something or someone has caused these "Lemon People" to wear a mask of bitterness. When you have to be around these people, make sure your gospel overrides their gossip. The gospel can be anything positive, the gossip is that which is negative. The following is an example:

Gossip: I hate my job. My boss is too demanding and my co – workers are snitches!!!

Gospel: I'm thankful to have a career. Even though there are problems, I never let them destroy my peace of mind.

So you have, in essence, said problems do exist, but you are still blessed to be employed. It has been said, "Attitudes are contagious. Is yours worth catching?" If you surround yourself with negative people (Lemon People), you will begin to sound like them. Furthermore, even if you listen to the gossip but don't engage in it, you are still an active participant in the negative communication process. For instance, when I was an educator, I would often eat lunch in the teacher's lounge and listen to a few of my colleagues degrade the students. Pretty soon, I too put in my two cents. I graduated from passive listener to active speaker and earned a diploma of stupidity and a degree of shame. Needless to say, I soon earned a Ph.D. in common sense and became absent from the lounge. I fellowshipped more with the positive colleagues; they truly lived as nurturers, and they outnumbered the few lemon teachers who soured the lounge.

It's so easy to fall into the trap of the Lemon People because we love to complain rather than exclaim. Positive people exclaim their trials and tribulations and work with vim, vigor and vitality to overcome. Positive people turn stumbling blocks into stepping-stones. Negative people (Lemon People) complain, but never seek to improve their condition. These individuals don't need your pity or approval. To validate their negative behavior or conversation is to destroy their potential for removing the sour disposition they possess. Whenever you are in their company, smile a lot. A warm smile can melt the coldest heart. Whenever you are in their company, ignore the negative gossip, but give a keen, sincere ear to the positive. Don't be afraid to be positive! You will get enough negative energy and conversation from external forces in your life, so you had better promote the positive. Those who spend the majority of their time in positive environments are the ones who have peace of mind. Peace of mind is essential if you are

to be a productive member of society. Because we too have down moments even as we inspire others, it is vital that we dwell in the company of those who will strengthen us when we are weak. "Pity Party" people, although popular to be around, leave us empty and often unfulfilled. Welcome constructive criticism and tough love. Choose the gospel over the gossip.

In our lives, there lies a purpose, a destiny, and an odyssey. However painful or unpopular it may be to family members, friends or acquaintances, release the Negative people from your internal space. You cannot always control the external forces, but you must seek to maintain the serenity of the internal. You deserve to be in a positive state of spiritual, economic, intellectual and social oneness. At this very moment, I dare you to be positive and a beacon of uplift. Every time you are in the company of lemon people, I dare you to be lemonade!!!

Thought: I will inhale and exhale the positive.

2
Fragile – Handle with Hair

It is not our mission to see through each other; it is our mission to see each other through.

Love is a universal word used in and by every race, creed and culture on the face of the earth. It has been celebrated in music, mayhem, and the media. It can be a kind gentle friend who sends warmth throughout our existence or masquerade as one, when we are left cold, empty and shivering because of it. Looking Over Various Experiences (LOVE), I have grown to realize Love must be handled with hair. Yes Hair!!! Sure the labels have traditionally said, "Fragile, Handle with care." The problem is that we are so careful with the contents within the box; we forget to handle with care once the box has been opened and the item put on display. This is so true in our relationships, especially our LOVE lives.

The aforementioned box is in our bodies; the contents include our hearts. Before we get to know each other, we are often loving, honorable and humble. In other words, we handle each other with care. This is true with relatives, co-workers, members in spiritual settings, friends and certainly in our Love lives. Once we become comfortable with each other, we somehow end up hurting those we Love the most. Jesus Christ illustrated the ultimate sacrifice of Love when He died for the sins and transgressions of the living, the dead and the unborn. That sacrifice will never be duplicated. We are God manifested beings of imperfection, and we will hurt – that's nature. Still, we can reduce the hurt if we simply handle with hair.

Hair is a commodity creatively styled by men and women in thousands of ways, and hundreds of methods are used to save it, especially through consumer marketing. Sadly, cancer patients lose their hair. As we age, we often lose our hair, and when we are stressed (usually in the name of Love), we tend to lose our hair. Quite often, because of lemon people in our lives, we lose more than our hair. We lose our self–esteem and in some cases, our sanity. Your heart is fragile, please handle it with hair. If relatives, co- workers, friends, church members and yes, boyfriends/girlfriends, husbands or wives are draining you physically, mentally, financially, emotionally and most essentially, spiritually, pray for them but don't stay for them. In other words, if their negative energy is too powerful and usurps your positive nature, you must release yourself or your heart and soul may not forgive you. Sometimes, the best way to love is from a distance. If they truly love you, they will alter their behavior. If not, by keeping your distance from them, you'll move closer to you.

And to all of you singles, genuinely, prayerfully and ardently seek a soul mate, not a roommate or playmate. You may want to re – think a wedding ring if you are presently enduring an abundance of suffering!!! I sincerely believe God has sent my soul mate to me, and the key to our Love is a mutual nurturing for one another.

The key to any love is mutual nurturing. Is that not what we strive to teach our children? Don't we encourage our children to, "Share, be nice, be a friend and you'll have friends?" You don't need an emotional dose of Rogaine. You just need to boldly regain that which you have lost over the years. The lemonade in you is more powerful than the lemons in others. If you allow yourself to become emotionally bald because of others, you may never become the blessing in someone else's life that God intended you to be.

At this moment, I dare you to remove your symbolic wig or toupee and take Love for what it is, **L**ooking **O**ver **V**arious **E**xperiences!!! These experiences will determine your future. Please handle with hair!!!

Thought: I will not pull out my hair. I will pull negative people out of my hair.

BIONIC
(Believe It Or Not I Care)
Dedicated to all of my children, regardless of race, creed or socioeconomic background.

YOUTH SKIT

Exclaimer #1: I live in the chaos of a confused society –
Where people wear mental shackles because they don't want to be free –
But I am emancipated and elevated, so when the enemy comes with a harmful dare –
I put on my BIONIC – Believe It Or Not I Care!

Exclaimer #2: Coogi, FUBU, Hilfiger, many are waiting on the next fad so they can feel bigger –

Dressing up their <u>behinds</u>, with nothing in their <u>minds</u> –
It's all about what they wear, but it's not what's on me; it's what's in me –
Believe It Or Not I Care!

Exclaimer #3: Respect, Responsibility and Righteousness, I do count as close friends –
In my generation, these qualities appear <u>rare</u> –
But I'm not a <u>thug</u> trying to pull a brotha's <u>plug</u> –
Believe It Or Not I <u>Care</u>!

Exclaimer #4: Many say the youth are out of <u>control</u> –
But whose example do we follow so <u>bold</u>?
I'm speaking the truth, so remove that shocked <u>stare</u>; adults are our role models –
Believe It Or Not, we watch and we <u>Care</u>!
Exclaimer #5: Regardless of my race, culture or <u>creed</u> –
I have a gift the world does <u>need</u> –
I will soar like an eagle in the air. Academics are a top priority –
Believe It Or Not I <u>Care</u>
Exclaimer #6: Never let anyone's negative opinion of you become your <u>reality</u> –
Never let the <u>enemy</u> keep you from reaching the <u>epitome</u> of your <u>destiny</u> –
What's wrong with you? Get up out of failure's <u>chair</u> –
Rise young <u>minds</u> and peace you will <u>find</u> –
Believe It Or Not, you must <u>Care</u>!
Exclaimer #7: It's not what people call <u>you</u>; it's what you chose to answer <u>to</u>!
Peer pressure is no excuse for us to be <u>oppressed</u>, <u>suppressed</u>, <u>repressed</u>, and <u>depressed</u> –

Keep your head <u>up</u>. Keep your coooooool – don't <u>erupt</u>!!!!

Exclaimer #8:   Tell all the negative ones to get to <u>steppin</u>; you don't need guns –

Your mind is your <u>weapon</u>.

Exclaimer #9:   You don't <u>need</u> <u>weed</u>!

Exclaimer #10: You never <u>dug</u> <u>drugs</u>!

Exclaimer #11: A <u>brew</u> cannot define <u>you</u>!

Exclaimer #12: Your mind and your heart are a powerful pair –

<u>Meditate</u> on your right to be <u>great</u> –

Believe It Or Not I <u>Care</u>

Believe It Or Not I…

Believe It Or Not…

Believe It Or…

Believe It…

Believe!!!!!

3

BIONIC
(Believe It Or Not I Care)

It is not our mission to see through each other; it is our mission to see each other through.

Everywhere you turn, our youth are being labeled Generation X! "X' simply means the unknown, and it usually has negative connotations. The truth is, however, many of our youth desire to exclaim their beauty, expand their minds and become excellent. Like many of us, our youth are stereotyped and categorized based on race, creed, and socioeconomic background. The falsehoods begin early, through word and action; we teach our children the following:

(A).   Sticks and stones may break my bones but words will never hurt.

(B).   Santa Claus, The Easter Bunny and The Tooth Fairy are more important than Christ and /or Parents.

(C).   If you don't wear name brand clothing, you are nothing.

(D).   Don't do as I do; do as I say do.

These four universal principles have helped to destroy many potential great minds and productive human beings of this generation. Names hurt far worse than sticks and stones. Words have power; they can build the soul or destroy the hearts core, leaving individuals empty and without purpose. Terms such as "nigga," "cracker," "ho" and "trick" are widely used by youth as both terms of misguided affection and degradation. Our youth need to be taught that a "nigga" (nigger) or "cracker" is the lowest form of the earth. A "nigga" has no self worth. A hoe is a garden utensil, and a "trick" is performed by a magician. We need not frown upon our youth; they learn these terms from us. As adults, we must expand our minds and our vocabularies. Names destroy self – esteem, and we often incorporate negative terms in our sense of being. Even in the midst of anger, we must work steadfast to refrain from using terms that are inhumane and down right cruel.

Santa Claus, The Easter Bunny, and the Tooth Fairy all have a place, but never should their importance out weigh spiritual or parental beings. Children must be taught that parents work hard to provide for them. Sure, give Santa Claus credit for a gift or two. There is nothing wrong with Rudolph, Frosty, or The Legend of Scrooge, but let the children know that hard working people who give gifts in the spirit and love of the greatest birth ever, the birth of Jesus Christ, purchased all gifts out of love. Corporate America and the media have an awesome task: Sell! Sell! Sell! They do this job very well, but parents cannot allow the toy industry to raise their children. The most vital task is keeping the Christ in Christmas (Christ – Mass). Furthermore, Santa only comes once a year. As a parent, you are there all the time. The resurrection of Christ must supercede the pagan history of the Easter Bunny at all costs. Even the seemingly harmless Tooth Fairy must not be the only source of recognition in a child's life. When these and other imaginary beings are allowed to be the primary forces in your children's lives, you are only preparing them to seek heroes outsideof their homes, schools, churches and communities.

Don't just dress up their behinds; put some knowledge in their minds. I don't have a problem with designer clothing. There's nothing wrong with wanting the best for your children. Make sure, however, that you don't outfit them to simply impress the masses or to simply increase your own pride. The danger in this is quite alarming. What happens when the child discovers that he/she is wearing the name of the top designer? If you can no longer afford designer X, what then? Today, many parents are ignoring mortgages, rent, vehicle notes and other bills so they can outfit their children with designer everything. Once again, children must be taught the value of clothing. The name on a shirt should not define the self – worth of an individual. Furthermore, love cannot be measured in materialism. Teaching them values is far more important than giving them valuables. Always seek to let their name be more significant than the name on their outfit. Refrain from buying things you don't need, with money you don't have, to impress people who don't care about you.

Out of fear, children will do as you say do. Out of respect, they will do as you do. The very nature of children and youth is to follow. Not surprisingly, that's the very nature of adults too. It's human nature. We can no longer be lemon people and expect our children and youth to be lemonade. Sure many will succeed in spite of our negative ways, but what about the thousands who look to us to pattern their lives after? I can only ask forgiveness for my many transgressions, and I've had to re–program my way of thinking so that the thousands of youth I speak to and mentor will be even thirstier for success and service.

This generation demands that we be more sincere than we have ever been. We have lost our fear of God and respect for each other, so our youth have lost respect for us. The media, schools, churches and government usually focus on the so – called troubled youth, but what about the so –called gifted youth? The fact is plain and simple: All of our youth are GIFTED! I was once labeled "special – education" material, at– risk, and a potential Menace to Society, but relatives taught me that I was special and gifted. Successful people in my churches taught me to take risks and people in the schools and communities taught me that with respect, responsibility, and resourcefulness, I could become amongst men who would ace society. These are the messages our youth desperately need today.

Moreover, we must be willing to learn their language, music and styles, not to appropriate or validate them, but to be able to relate to these creative young minds. This will only open the dialogue between youth and adults. We must have the courage to teach them that being BI – lingual is fine, depending on the setting:

Lunch cafeteria: Yo man, pass me the grub so I can get my eat on!

Formal banquet: Excuse me; please pass the food because I'm quite hungry.

Sure it sounds funny, but communication can make or break you in a society. The following list may help you better understand today's youth:

Da bomb – Successful

Boo – Boyfriend/girlfriend

Chillin – Relaxing

Dope – Beautiful

Off the Chain – Super

Beef – A problem

Mac daddy – Playboy

Bout it – Agree with it

Ho, Trick, Skeezer – Negative terms for females

Bust A Cap – Shoot Someone

Props – Compliments, rewards

I'm Down – I agree

True Dat – I understand

Slow Ya Roll – calm down

The Read – Information

Crunk – Exciting

Fronting – Pretending

Fu-sho – Definitely

Tight – Good

Buggin/Trippin – Crazy

Dog – Friend

There are hundreds more, but these are some of the common ones. You may not approve of them, but it helps to know that if someone says, "I'll bust a cap in you," he/she is not talking about a soda top. You're about to be shot. Furthermore, these terms are not restricted to one particular group or race of youth.

Extra! Extra! Read All About It

Sticks and Stones didn't hurt Eric Harris and Dylan Klebold's bones, but being called names such as "fag" did. These two intelligent young men created a virtual bloodbath at Columbine high School on **April 20, 1999**. On **October 1, 1997**, Luke Woodham, 16 of Pearl, Mississippi, killed his mother, three high school classmates and wounded seven others. On **December 1, 1997** Michael Carnel, 14 of West Paducah, Kentucky, killed three students at an early Morning Prayer meeting. On **March 24,1998**, Mitchell Johnson, 13 and

Andrew Golden, 11 of Jonesboro, Arkansas set off a fire alarm and then killed four students and a teacher. On **May 21, 1998** Kip Kinkel, 15 of Springfield, Oregon killed his parents and shot 24 students at school, two of which died.

These horrific incidents nearly shattered the fiber of America. These seven young men, ages 11 – 18 all had several of the same traits: Young, gifted and white. These incidents have been chronicled as some of the worse in U.S. history, and downright shocking and unbelievable. The May 3, 1999 issue of Newsweek Magazine did an excellent job illustrating "The Science of Teen Violence" and "Why the Young Kill." Although the latter part of the 90's produced such gloom and doom events, I simply ask, "Were we as a nation shocked by the events, or by who caused them?'"

Where was the national attention when youth of color were being murdered on school grounds nationwide? Furthermore, why did everyone ignore the warning signs at Columbine a year before the tragedy? Eric and Dylan waved a gun at a student in the neighborhood. They made a video pretending to shoot fellow classmates. Teachers and parents warned the authorities that they were violent, and Eric had a web site with the quote "Kill em AALLLL!!!" No one paid attention.

The facts are mind-boggling. We have grouped our youth into two categories: At – Risk (minorities, especially black males) and Low –Risk, (white youth, especially white males). This stereotyping is tragic but real. If we are to save our youth, we must nurture all of them. Even when it is those in our social circles, we must acknowledge that they too can be potentially dangerous. Danger and violence are not racial in nature. They are human in nature. As a nation, we have been programmed to believe young black males in particular and minorities in general, are the only ones who commit violent acts. Thus, these individuals live in a defensive mode under a magnifying glass like laboratory rats. If we are to save our youth, we must teach them the values of respect, responsibility, tolerance and compassion. If we are to save our youth, we must promote diversity. If we are to save our youth, we must stop allowing the television to raise them. We must get our youth involved in extra – curricular activities. I was involved in so many as a teen; I was too tired to get into trouble. We must realize that there is good and bad in hip – hop, rock, heavy metal and video games. We must listen to our youth's Universal cry for acceptance and attention. Moreover, we must channel those cries into constructive means rather than destructive ones. If we want to release the greatness in our youth, we too must adhere to the same principles we beckon them to live by.

At this very moment, I dare you to look in the mirror and remember both the troubled and triumphant teen in you, and then become the adult who gave hope to that same teen who stares back.

Thought: I will work diligently to help Generation X become Generation Excellent.

4

Hide and Seek

*It is not our mission to see through each other; it is our
mission to see each other through.*

As children, we all played hide and seek. We scattered
wildly as the chosen one would count one to ten and search for
us in those secret places that gave us sweet serenity in the midst
of the chaos. We were young then, and our problems were
reduced to, "Mother May I," "Red Light, Green Light 1,2,3,"
"Duck, Duck, Goose," and running behind the Ice cream truck.
We focused on ourselves and took time to laugh. We were
innocent then, and we were "real" with ourselves and others.
We relaxed because we chose to. It's time to allow the child in
you to come out and play again.

You are so bogged down with your marriage, children,
career, church, organizations and other events of the world,
you have forgotten that Calgon (women) or Octagon (men)
exists. It's time for you to take at least one hour out of each day
to play hide and seek. ONE HOUR! That's only 7 hours per
week out of 168. Sleep does not count because you're usually
dreaming about people, places or events. Your hide and seek
time should be the time during the day when you are

transformed into a turtle (slow and tucked away inside your
shell). During this hour, you must receive no correspondence
by phone or in person. You must relax, meditate, and watch
your favorite television show (alone), exercise, read or perform
any stress reliever that you can do alone. Don't allow anyone or
anything to invade your space. Your hide and seek is a mission
of self uplift and "Maintain the Sane." You must seek to grow
during your time alone. Connect with the Creator and reflect on
happiness.

If you neglect yourself because of life's rat race, you'll
realize even after the race is finished, you're still a rat. You can
give all of your time to others and be rotten, angry and timid or
give time to yourself and be relaxed, angelic and tenacious.
Which "rat" will you be in this race called life? It has been
said, "We make our living by what we get: we make our lives
by what we give." This is so true. In addition to everyone's
agenda for you, you must have an itinerary safely tucked away
in your heart, mind and soul. Don't be afraid or guilty because
of a desire to manifest self – preservation. This world will not
miss you for an hour a day. In fact, others may discover a
greater sense of independence. So even as you commune with
yourself, you are indeed enhancing the lives of others. Ready or
not...

At this very moment I dare you to schedule you at least one
hour per day. I dare you to hide and seek peace of mind.

*Thought: I will hug myself at least once a day, seeking to
hide away in the warmth of me.*

5
Super – Vision not Supervision

It is not out mission to see through each other; it is our mission to see each other through.

Many people in society are excelling in their chosen professions, prospering because their super – vision has come into fruition. So many more, however, are on jobs where they are sick and tired of being sick and tired. They have relied on someone else's supervision of them rather than a super – vision for themselves. In reality, you have three risk levels: low – risk, medium – risk, and high – risk. If you desire to change careers and you are single with no children or married with no children, you are at the low – risk level. If you are a single parent, depending on your salary – you are either at the medium or high – risk level. If you are married with children, the same applies to you. Regardless of your marital status, you need to feel totally fulfilled in your profession (economically, professionally, etc…). You need to feel like you are an essential piece of the professional puzzle. If not, you will find yourself in a workplace maze of despair.

From 1994 – 99, I was blessed to be an English, Drama and Speech educator at East Laurens High School in Dublin, Georgia. My students were essential to my life – line. I was a full time educator, surrogate father, and a part – time motivational speaker. My vision had always been to uplift the masses through motivational speaking, writing, and consulting. I was, therefore, living out a portion of my vision. In 1998, however, the super – vision that was planted in my spirit began to sprout at an alarming rate, and in 1999, I became a full – time motivational speaker. There were those who attempted to provide kind supervision by telling me to stay put, but the super – vision had manifested itself. The results have been mind – boggling thus far. Under supervision, I was able to inspire and be inspired by 700 students and colleagues, but under my super – vision, I've directly inspired and been inspired by over 20,000 people (primarily youth) in less than two years! Furthermore, my God – given super – vision has inspired many of my former students to seek a super – vision, rather than supervision.

When you have a dream, vision or goals, don't share them with everyone. One negative comment by the lemon people may destroy your aspirations. Furthermore, if you do share them, don't get upset or angry if people don't share your enthusiasm. Your purpose in life is uniquely yours, and if you don't fulfill it, it may not come to pass. The supervisors or supervision in our lives may say, "Play it safe." "Don't take risks." "Better safe than sorry." Well, you'll be sorry if you always play it safe. God saw enough in you to create you, so you must see enough in your potential to do great works that will enhance the human race as well as you personally.

If you are presently in a career – field and know you won't change, but have a desire to do something more, make time to do it. Remember that I was an educator and public speaker before I decided to "Step out on Faith" as a full – time speaker. You can have your career and manifest your super – vision as well if they are not synonymous. For example, you may work for a state agency from 9 to 5 under supervision, but during two evenings per week, you sing melodiously at a Jazz café under your super – vision. You may work at a local convenience store under supervision, but on your days off, you manage a daycare under your super – vision. The possibilities are endless. Whatever you are presently doing under supervision, also seek a super – vision in another area of your life, even if that area is only a hobby. You have a gift that only you can unwrap. There are thousands of business opportunities in society, opportunities for ownership. Even if none are right for you, create your own. You deserve to prosper and be totally fulfilled.

Those who seek to utilize all of their God – given gifts are the ones who will reap spiritual, economic, cultural, social, and intellectual freedom. Remember that the lemon people in life will never take this bold step, and if you listen to their negative communication instead of manifesting your super – vision, you won't either.

At this very moment, I dare you to have 20/20 vision when it comes to your super – vision!

Thought: It is my decision to embrace my super – vision!

6

"Equally Yolked – Not Rotten Eggs"

It is not our mission to see through each other; it is our mission to see each other through.

He: Let's grow spiritually, economically, physically, culturally and socially.

She: Let's respect, reflect and protect each other.

He: Let's hold, mold and gently scold each other.

She: Let's excite, delight and ignite each other.

He: Let's agree to disagree and still be in love!

She: Let's be side by side and allow faith and forgiveness to abide.

Pause…this is not a fairytale. If you are in a relationship with a significant other you should closely mirror the he/she dialogue. It is brief, yet broad and bold. In this New Millennium, you must be equally yolked, not rotten eggs! When you are yolked, you have good times and bad moments, not vice versa. When you are equally yolked, you don't <u>go</u> through things; you <u>grow</u> through things because you both have high expectations and aspirations. If your significant other, however, is a lemon person, you might want to consider the following:

(A).   Will this person ultimately cause me to lose my sanity?

(B).   Can I be comfortable bringing him/her around family and friends?

(C).   Does he/she want to work?

(D).   Is there emptiness after the physical?

(E).   Is he/she going to get spiritually connected one day?

(F).   Is this the person I want my child to call Mom/Dad?

(G).   Does he/she build or lower my self – esteem?

You can answer one question one day at a time for exactly one – week. Write a brief summary or a full – page report after each answer. Evaluate and re – evaluate because after your relationship with God, the relationship with your significant other will be most vital.

I sincerely believe that the misconceptions about relationships are established early on. We tend to choose individuals by two basic criteria: What we want and/or what we need. Both of these can lead to you ending up with a rotten egg instead of someone you're equally yolked with. Remember when you were a child and you "needed" to eat vegetables to grow, but you resented them. Furthermore, you "wanted" a lot of dessert, but it often gave you a stomachache. Relationships are the same way. If you listen to people who tell you what type of person you "need," even if the significant other is a quality individual, you may resent your mate. Moreover, if you choose a person solely on what you want (usually fueled by physical or materialistic attributes), you may end up used and abused for sacrificing your dignity to get what you <u>think</u> you want!

No one ever talks about the third option: What You Deserve! That is the key. You were made in an image so omnipotent, omnipresent, and omniscient – you DESERVE the best! Your wants and/or your needs are quite secondary to the primary issue: What you DESERVE! You deserve someone who can uplift you in every phase of your life. You deserve someone who can <u>come in</u> when it appears the whole world has <u>gone out</u>!

You deserve someone who wants greatness not mediocrity. You deserve someone who will listen to you and not laugh at your dreams, goals, and visions. You deserve someone who your children can model themselves after. You deserve someone whose touch sends a rush through your body, mind, and soul like a vigorous volcano or turbulent thunderstorm! You deserve the epitome of ecstasy, and it can all be yours! You must first, however, make sure you possess many of the qualities you seek in your significant other.

Many married couples are not soul mates. They are merely roommates. Many others seeking to one day tie the knot have too much suffering, so they need not exchange wedding rings. Many more are simply hanging on because of habit, slowly becoming symbolic hard-boiled rotten eggs locked in a shell. There are, however, couples of a positive "equally yolked" mentality. Their spirit cannot be broken. What the world labels as problems, they classify as situations. They are prosperous spiritually, economically, and socially. They are not perfect, but they know What They Deserve!

Wherever you are in your relationship, seek genuine happiness. You won't find it in the physical only! You won't find it in being absorbed in self or by being right all the time. Genuine happiness is a state of mind, an attitude, and a way of life.

At this moment, I dare you to be happy in your relationship, not based on wants or needs but on What You Deserve!

He: Let's grow spiritually, economically, physically, culturally and socially.

She: Let's respect, reflect and protect each other.

He: Let's hold, mold and gently scold each other.

She: Let's excite, delight and ignite each other.

He: Let's agree to disagree and still be in love!

She: Let's be side by side and allow faith and forgiveness to abide.

Thought: *I deserve a soul mate not a playmate or a roommate.*

7

Seven Sensational Days

*It is not our mission to see through each other; it is our
mission to see each other through.*

All of our lives, we've been taught and programmed to
allow our attitudes, emotions and spirits to mirror the so –
called mood of the days of the week. Sunday has been a
universal day of worship and rest. Sunday evening, however,
leads to the gloom, which carries us into the "Miserable
Monday." We sleepwalk through Monday and head into
terrible Tuesday. Like Monday, it's still the beginning of the
week. On "Wacky Wednesday," we wake up and realize that
it's "humpday," and we're almost back to the weekend. We
become thirsty for Thursday and its enamored ending. Finally,
we exclaim, "Thank God it's Friday." On Saturday, we are free
to release the stress of Monday – Friday. Saturday belongs to
us! In essence, we have reduced Seven Sensational Days to two
of sweet serenity. The stress, however, of the other five will
dominate and seemingly shorten the other two if we don't re –
program our thought process.

Each day we must wake up and exclaim, "Today, I choose
life, not strife." "I am too blessed to be stressed."

Monday

It's a magnificent, marvelous, magical Monday. It's the start of a new week. The outlook shall not be bleak. I will be positive in all I do and speak. New horizons I will seek. On this day, I will reach a new peak!

Tuesday

It's terrific, tremendous Tuesday. Monday is gone and I'm still motivated. My attitude will cause others to be stimulated. No situation will cause me to be deflated. I will inhale all of the positives that are stated. Hello Tuesday – It's the two of us together we will soar!

Wednesday

It's wonderful Wednesday. Tuesday is a distant memory. Wednesday it's just you and me. In the week, you stand in the center. Today, I'll uplift someone and be a mentor. Today I will welcome Wednesday's splendor!

Thursday

It's tantalizing, thankful Thursday. I left Wednesday in my dreams. Today, I will rise to the top like cream. I will promote the concept of TEAM. I embrace you Thursday – we're headed upstream.

Friday

It's fantastic, favorable Friday. Thursday took me places. On today I'll put smiles on many faces. I will dismiss all negative cases. And welcome love in all hollow spaces! Welcome Weekend!! I deserve you!!

Yes, you deserve the weekend, but you also deserve to be happy during the week also. At this moment, I dare you to live for seven sensational days, not just two. I dare you to allow your week and weekends to merge into one cohesive unit of peace and prosperity.

Quotable Quotes
By:
"Preacher"

A -   "Religion has become a fad. Spirituality is a focus."

B -   "There's nothing wrong with freedom, but it's dumb not to want to be free."

C -   "If they must be labeled Generation X, let's teach them to exclaim their beauty,
        expand their minds and be excellent!"

D -   "The same system that says don't discipline the children is the same exact one
        building more prisons than schools to discipline and devour them."

E -   "Many in America say we must reason with our children. That's the reason we're in
        this predicament today."

F -   "I went from being labeled Special – Ed. To being special, at – risk to taking risks
        and a menace to society to dwell among men who aced society."

G -   "Pray for negative people, but don't stay for negative people. They will only kill your spirit."

H -   "You don't need supervision. You need a super – vision."

I -   "We must seek to maintain the Sane."

J -   "It is time to reflect each other, protect each other and connect each other."

8
Choices vs. Voices

It is not our mission to see through each other; it is our mission to see each other through.

The voice of others will take your vision and smear <u>it</u>.
The choice is to obey your inner voice and your inner <u>spirit</u>.
The voice of others will demand that you hear <u>it</u>.
The choice is to listen to your inner voice and sincerely
   endear <u>it</u>.
The voice of others can heal you or cut you like a <u>knife</u>.
The choice is listen to the voices of others and have a
   living or obey your voice and have a <u>life</u>.
Advice comes knocking on our door on a daily basis, and
chooses family members, friends, co – workers and others
as accomplices. How many times have we heard the phrase,
"Can I give you a bit of advice?"
You're probably shaking your head right now because
   someone has said it to you within the last 24 hours.
Advice has undoubtedly come from a warm, welcomed
friend, and a cold calculating enemy during your lifetime.
Remember the time your wise grandmother said, "Don't go
out, I have a funny feeling about tonight?" You heard her
<u>voice,</u> but the choice was yours to make. On that particular
night you decided not to go, and the next morning you were
relieved. Your best friend called to say that someone who
chose to drink and drive had been fatally injured in the car

you were supposed to ride in. On one hand, you feel awful because you believe you could have caused that person to change his/her mind about drinking and driving. On the other hand, you are relieved because you are alive. Remember the guy or girl your parents told you not to date? You did it anyway and ended up emotionally battered. Or perhaps you did not and this person ended up being a kind, compassionate, successful person. We have all experienced these and hundreds of other scenarios in our lives. It appears that everyone knows what's best for us except us!

Voices

Many of us have heard, but were we listening? The voices are not the ones inside of you. The voices are the ones around you. At some point in your life, you are going to have to make independent decisions. The voices may be heard, but you should listen to your inner voice. Many times, the voices that surround us have their own perceptions and ideas of who or what we should be. For a long time, I have heard the following from well-meaning loving voices: Keith, you are going to be a Preacher. You ought to be a Preacher. You sound like a Preacher. The voices are valid in their realm of being, but only my voice will validate my mission. Furthermore, God has made me a motivational speaker. He has spoken to my spirit. You don't have to be what the voices see you as. Just be productive in whatever path you choose, and be certain your path uplifts others in some way, shape or form. The voices do not know your destiny. Each individual is given a unique gift, and no one knows that but him or her.

Furthermore, some people never realize what the omnipotent voice is saying, so how can someone else who did not create me be the authority on a path in life for someone else? If this sounds a bit harsh, look around at all the unhappy campers who allow someone else's voice to govern their lives. They are merely content with surviving on someone else's voice. You Too Have A Voice.

The voices also have a habit of living their dreams through others. This is quite evident between parents and children, older and younger siblings and other relatives. Parents, guardians, and relatives – Don't force your voices on our youth. Let your voices be those of support and encouragement. As long as the dreams promote goals which are realistic, support them. I'm below average in Mathematics, so there was no way I was going to excel as an Engineer. I always dreamed of being an actor, so my parents used their voices to promote my aspirations. Moreover, they enrolled me in theatre productions, and made certain I participated in church plays, community theatre and school plays. When I became an adult, I chose to teach high school drama and speech, and although I'm not an actor, I'm still using my voice to uplift the masses. At some point, my inner voice had to supercede the voices of others, especially those that were discouraging and degrading. We will all have to deal with voices that minimize our worth. These voices have one purpose and one purpose only: To ensure that we don't maximize our God – given gifts. When we allow these voices to become primary, we end up as secondary beings with low self – esteem and no voice. Yes reader, the voices are here, and they are not going away. In the midst of all the voices, you must seek to go to the next level: CHOICES!

Choices

The life you live must be one of choice not chance. The choices in life are difficult, but you must choose your path. The only voice that should <u>totally</u> guide you is the Omnipotent Voice of the Creator. I've made negative choices in life; they hurt deeply, but they would have been more tragic had I allowed the voices of others to override my inner voice. I must point out that if an inner voice beckons you to commit an illegal, immoral or unethical act, you must work steadfast to ignore it. Your inner voice will seek redemption through sincere repentance. Choices are the difference between success and failure, happiness and sadness and life and death. Don't let the voices of others be the deciding factor in your choices. There's nothing wrong with seeking advice, but don't let advice silence your inner voice. If you don't recognize the power of your own inner voice to make choices, you will always be manipulated by the choices others will make for you.

You will make both good choices and bad ones, but the good ones will remind you of how much you need to learn from the bad ones. You are not perfect reader, and neither are the voices that seek to guide your every move in life. The stage has been set! The time is now! Your choices can be positive and universally uplifting.

At this very moment I dare you to make the choice to listen to your inner voice.

Thought: The voices of the world are fine, but the ultimate choice is to listen to the one that is mine.

9
Miracles not Miracle Whip

It is not our mission to see through each other; it is our mission to see each other through.

There I sat – in a euphoria that sex, money, materialistic items, nor the confirmation of a speaking engagement could give me. And if I drank or used drugs, I'm sure neither could compete with the "high" that I felt as I sat drenched in tears that flowed like Niagara Falls. I thought to myself, "God why here? Why now?" Suddenly, I had to shout hallelujah, and this chapter was born out of the womb of peace and prosperity: God provides Miracles not Miracle Whip.

I sincerely believe networking through oral communication is a vital key for recognizing God's miracles. Even when you read a book, you should be able to hear the writer's voice as you read his/her words of expression. When you come upon someone, and he/she shows you love, even in the midst of his/her pain, he/she is exemplifying God's miracle at work. However, when you come upon someone who gives off negative vibes or makes you feel unworthy to be in his/her presence, that's miracle whip – and the longer you stay in this environment, the more whipped you will be. Miracle Whip is so tempting. It's good for the moment, just like the sandwich spread. Miracle Whip is only temporary.

Miracle Whip adds flavor and spice to your life. It can come in three forms: People, things or ideas. The key point to ponder and then remember is quite uncomfortable: God is not the author and finisher of Miracle Whip. He is the author and finisher of Miracles!!!!! People who love to gossip with us all the time are keen examples of Miracle Whip. We sit with them, spread the gossip on thick, and then eat away at the lives of others. The sandwich is so tasty, but it is hard to digest because those who gossip with us will soon gossip about us. What we fail to realize though is that while we are in a Miracle Whip state of mind and communication, God will use His Miracle working power to uplift those same individuals who we have chosen to judge. Furthermore, the Miracle He had for us will be blocked by the Miracle Whip. We can't receive His blessings, his wonders, and His Miracles because we are so consumed by Miracle Whip.

Moreover, Miracle Whip has us believing that when we acquire homes, vehicles, money, and expensive clothing, we are supposed to praise these materialistic things. Miracle Whip has a clever concept: Show off your goods your goods so that others will see how God is! Oh Yes, Miracle Whip is spread on thick. The truth of the matter, however, is as follows: Let your humble manner and glory to God Illustrate to others how they can attain Miracles!!! WARNING!!! Do not be ashamed to have material wealth. You deserve it as an heir of the omnipotent one, but don't gloat either. Don't be whipped. Be watchful, for that which was given to you can be removed from you without warning or explanation. I must admit that I have been whipped by my ideas. "I believe this... I feel... In my opinion..." And people applauded. At times they felt beneath me because I was considered "deep." My ideas left me whipped, and I missed out on some Miracles because I placed my trust in man instead of the God who created the man. My ideas led me to be whipped by the following: It's not what you know; it's who you know. I was whipped into believing that if I belittled myself to man, I would be elevated. In other words, God could not emancipate me with Miracles because I was knee deep in passiveness, and reactive-ness!!! I have been Miracle Whipped by many other ideas and so have you, but if we sincerely desire to be blessed, we must get our directions from the director. We must embrace His ideas and let ours be a reflection of His. You will make mistakes, and you will get Miracle Whipped; however, make certain you only get the sandwich and not become a full party platter!

Now back to those tears that ran down my cheeks. I must say "Hallelujah" once again. I cried and cried and cried some more, and God had the angels bottle my tears and place them in spiritual storage.

I wept with joy as I thought about Marcus Howell, a young black male. A spiritual young black male – not a <u>nigga</u> (misguided socially appropriate term for nigger). Menace to Society – No! Marcus is a true SOLDIER (Standing On Love Dignity Intelligence, Excellence and Righteousness). On December 3, 2000, Marcus was in a near fatal car accident that left him partially paralyzed. When I visited him in Shepherd's Spinal Clinic in Atlanta, Georgia, he was in a wheelchair, but his spirit and his smile lit my heart with a flame of Miracle proportions. Marcus is a Miracle of God, and he refuses to be whipped. He knows he will walk again, just as others have. He will not be whipped; he gave me a new purpose for living. Like Marcus, the patients of Shepherd's are Miracles.

And then there was Valerie Williams. Valerie was shot in the head by her ex – husband. She was supposed to die, by medical standards. God would not allow Val to be whipped. She went through physical and psychological terror; the first time she looked into the mirror after the shooting, she thought she was Frankenstein's monster. All had been ripped and stripped from her. Her so-called soul mate attempted to take her life and soul. Today, however, five years after her near death experience, Val has completed her book <u>God's Divine Intervention</u>. When I met Valerie and heard her story, I wept. She said my motivational speaking touched and inspired her. I thought, "My God, you have inspired me without saying a single word." I cannot forget little Jasmine Seaborn, "God's Anointed One." I met Jasmine at a Christmas party for Miracle Children, those inflicted with Sickle Cell Anemia. Jasmine is blind, but she sees far better than many of us with physical sight. Jasmine has appeared on Showtime at the Apollo," The Disney Channel and other venues. She has a gospel CD on the market, and she's a top – notch student. Jasmine's Miracle Spirit rubbed off on me. As I pondered what I would say to the audience at the Christmas party, Jasmine touched me and said, "You're blessed, don't think too hard. Use what God gave you." Hallelujah – I delivered a fun – filled, soul – stirring message of hope thanks to the God in a Miracle named Jasmine. You are too a Miracle. I am a miracle. The system once labeled me Special – Ed., At – Risk and a potential Menace to Society. I was by all counts, whipped. However, God transformed the Special – Ed label to "Gifted." With support from family, church and community members, I was able to take risks, and because of the soul mate God has blessed me with, I must become among men who will ace society. Like you, I've had to ask God to turn lessons into blessings. We need not be whipped any longer. God has something much, much, much more genuine for us.

At this very moment, I dare you to hang with Miracles. I dare you to embrace your Miracles. I dare you to stop being whipped!

Thought: When the Miracle Whip calls me, I will ignore it and be bold! When the miracle touches me, I will embrace it in my soul!

10
Not By Sperm – By Spirit

*It is not our mission to see though each other; it is our
mission to see each other through.*

I was 9 years old and it was the fall of my 5th grade year.
This was 1978, a time when there was no cursing in cartoons,
no violence in video games, and "Our Gang" was a figurative
term for mocking Spanky, Buckwheat, Alfalfa and Darla's
antics on the <u>Little Rascals</u>. On this particular evening,
Mommy's cherry pie was illuminating the house with a scent
that could only be rivaled by the funnel cake stand at the local
carnival. I had just finished bathing, and the Planet of the Apes
was victorious over GI Joe's army in the bathtub version of
World War II. It was 6:00p.m. and in the Jordan home that
meant two things: Daddy's almost home and the start of New
York's infamous Eyewitness News with Ernie Anastos and
Spencer Christian. It also meant a retreat for me to my humble
abode, filled with <u>Star Wars</u> artifacts everywhere and a poster of
Reggie Jackson of the Yankees and the New York Knicks.

Because of the sound of the airplanes that periodically
hovered over our house like eagles on a mission, I often missed
out on the sounds of the house. On this night, I missed the
entrance of the 5'6" staunch, handsome, noble creature called
"Daddy" by Regina and I and Charles by my mom. He always
looked so dignified in his blue uniform, with its TA symbol
(Transit Authority) as well as his army fatigues. Still, he was
always exhausted when he arrived home. But he was never too

tired to hug each member of his family, and he always said to me, "Boo, how was your day?" I earned the name "Boo" several years earlier during a restroom escapade. Then came the dreaded question; Boo, Did you do your homework??? And on this night, with my Atari Video Game "Pac Man" waiting on pause, I blundered, "Yes, Daddy." And then my entire world sank like Satchel Paige's slider; my daddy said, "Let me check it." I knew then that Pac Man and I would have to hook up another time. Mrs. Finkelstein, my 5th grade nurturing nemesis, had won again. After carefully going over my errors, my dad called my mom in the room and said, "Gertrude, we have to change Boo's schedule after school – Check all his homework before he goes outside, watches television or plays Atari." My eyes swelled with tears, and I knew Mommy empathized with me. I was sent to my room. I know my parents had a lively discussion, but when all was said and done, my new schedule was in tact.

On that fall day of 1978, the man the world called my "step – dad," had saved a great portion of my life and the woman whose womb I exited did not fight his decision. I was a mama's boy, so naturally anything that made me sad saddened her, even if my sadness was child manipulation to divide my parents. On that day, my father, not by sperm – by spirit gave me a new lesson in responsibility. He didn't yell at me or spank me. He gave me directions and I followed them. Twenty – three years later, my dad's example of "LOVE" still helps me stay focused.

Early on…it was quite difficult, especially for my beautiful, honorable, humble mother. She and my biological father did not end up together with a home, two – car garage, children, a dog and yearly trips to Disney World. They were and still are two wonderful human beings; however, it is very realistic for two good people not to be good for each other. I still don't know the reason behind the demise, just as you don't know about hidden, deep, dark secrets about your existence and family, yet out of the darkness comes light, a Shekinah Glory. Out of the supposed mess, there is a profound <u>message</u>!!!

My mom was caught in a catch – 22 situation, as many single mothers are. For years, they labor and nurture their children, not in father – less homeless homes but in mother – more homes. They are given assistance and much advice from family members, primarily grandparents who always speak and live as if they know "what's best for the child." Loving, caring, uplifting family members have also shown themselves to be over bearing, and too opinionated. My mom faced this when God sent Charles E. Jordan into her life. He had four children of his own, but my mother married him because he possessed both the strength and serenity she was looking for and God knew she deserved it. She became a mother of 5 at the tender age of 29 and suddenly I had two dads.

Between the ages of 4 and 8, I lived the life of an exchange student. I went from New York to Savannah, Savannah to New York, New York to Savannah, and Savannah to New York. The moves had a great deal to do with how my father by spirit thought I should be raised vs. how my mother thought I should be raised. My father by spirit believed in staunch discipline, not abuse. He believed in making me responsible at a young age. I was a Mama's boy and often I played my parents against each other. In other words, I was a child. My mother's family believed in discipline too, but I was able to get away with much more because I was "little Keithy," a precious child who did no wrong. But in 1976, the North to South – South to North journeys ceased. At the end of my 3rd grade year, I was labeled and headed to Special – Ed.!!!

This time, New York would become my permanent home, and my father by spirit was able to mold me into a fine young man. My mother allowed him to love me, discipline me and his discipline kept me off the streets and possibly out of prison or an early grave. His love gave me confidence and security. His example of husband hood, fatherhood, and manhood has given me life – long pride and a blueprint as I begin my journey as a father by spirit and husband!

I'm thankful for all four of my parents, actually six (Theodore and Betty Richardson, an uncle and aunt who served as guardians during each summer of my childhood, adolescence and beyond). I must also salute my Mama Ginia (short for Virginia) and Mama Lillie (deceased), grandmothers who sacrificed so much for me. My godmother Louise was such a blessing to me. My family was and is awesome. Yes I cried many nights wondering why I had two dads, two moms, brothers and sisters on both sides, and a partridge in a pear tree. But you too have cried many nights over an aspect of your childhood. I'm thankful for Carolyn Brown, the wonderful woman whose womb I did not evolve from, yet she still gave me an abundance of warmth. I'm Thankful for my biological father Ted "Pieback" Brown. He has taught me how to network and be a people's person. I can't dwell on the past; however, questions will always remain. I would be lost without Gertrude Jordan, the royal womb that produced me. She has sacrificed so much just so I could obtain a sense of happiness and purpose. And God knows I'm thankful for the man who came in and made me his son. Society calls him a step – father! Oh yes, he stepped right in and allowed God to use him so that I could become Keith "Preacher" Brown, the motivator of the Millennium.

To God be the glory for re – writing my story. Perhaps you are in a similar situation, where the spirit outweighed the sperm or the warmth replaced the womb. Perhaps you too have hordes of questions running through your mind. Believe it or not, those individuals whose parents stayed together have the same questions. We all have dysfunctional areas in our blood – line. We all want the answers to so many questions or do we? At this point in my life, the answers won't matter because God has not allowed me to stand still. Each mistake has produced His mercy. He has allowed me to shout "Hallelujah" through all of the pain. This I do know – Had my biological parents made it, I would never have experienced the warmth of Charles Jordan. I wouldn't have experienced being a little brother to Dwight, going to all of his track meets, pledging his fraternity, listening to all of his advice even when he thought I wasn't. I wouldn't have been pampered by Cheryl, who often acted as my mother. I wouldn't have been able to hang with Regina; fighting over whose turn it was to clean the house. I wouldn't have been able to receive applause from Phyllis after each new dance move. There would have been no older siblings! I would not have seen the birth and growth of Caryn and Tykeisha, my two little sisters – one from each biological parent. And yes, we all have experienced some type of pain as a result of our stories, but I must reflect on the positive aspects because the pen is now in my hand. Much of my story was written for me, but God has given me inspirational ink and I must write a story that is worthy of His Son's ultimate sacrifice. Just to look back evokes a plethora of emotions, the same emotions that you feel right now reader.

I am moved to tell single mom's and dad's the following: If God places a Charles Jordan or Carolyn Brown in your life, embrace that individual and pray, pray and pray some more.

Allow that person to help you raise your child(ren) in a positive way, utilizing love and discipline. Do not allow your family members to separate you from God's gift to you, and make your child(ren) feel important but not superior to you or your sent helpmate. Remember though, the helpmate must be God sent and not "Your sent" or "Mama sent" or Daddy sent" or "Friend sent," etc... The key is prayer and meditation. Another profound aspect is realizing why you are a single parent in the first place. If by death to the other parent, you had no control. However, if you got caught up with a masked fool (a man or woman disguised as being focused and reliable), you need to do a serious self – examination to make sure you are fixed before you seek companionship elsewhere. And by all means, make sure you and the other biological parent have severed all ties (except for discussions pertaining to the welfare of the child (ren); And your heartstrings left over must be cut before you enter into a new realm of romance with anyone.

In other words, all "Baby daddy/mama drama" needs to be dead and buried. If you can't move on, don't allow anyone else to move into your life. It won't be fair to that person or your child (ren).

Reader, the inspirational ink is now your pen. The story you decide to write will be uniquely yours. It won't matter whether you come from an environment with both biological parents, one biological parent, adoptive parents, foster parents, step – parents or surrogate parents. What will matter is how your spirit stands up next to the sperm.

Now I prepare to be a husband to my soul mate Wakea, a spiritual, beautiful surrogate mother to her students and biological mother to Keon. My sperm did not produce him, but my spirit will decide much of his success or failure. God is already manifesting my spirit in his daily actions. Someone is waiting on your spirit to help him/her grow.

At this very moment, I dare you to allow the spirit to supercede the sperm. Quite often the sperm complex in our families pretends all will be well and the years will heal all. The spirit, however, beckons us to communicate, meditate, and motivate. If we don't, the years will change but the wounds won't. I dare you to embrace the spirit!

Thought: I survived one out of thousands of sperm, and the inner spirit will not allow me to be a societal germ!!!

Mother More

The following is a tribute to Gertrude Jordan – my Mother,
the one who always sought to keep confusion out of the mix,
often times sacrificing her own happiness!!!!!!

Mother of the earth, born out of a rib
Now the backbone of civilization
For so many years you have been the mule
And we abused the richness of your soil
Calling you all things but a child of God.

Mama breastfed other people's children
Mama cooked for other people's children
Mama cleaned up other people's houses
Mama had to milk other people's cows
Mama toiled the land of other people
Then you came home and breastfed your child
Then cooked pigs feet for your family
Without Pine Sol, you made your house smell fresh
Your last dollar bought some milk and oatmeal
Your glowing smile fertilizes the land

You sucked the blood from my infested knee
You wiped me when I could not wipe myself
You spanked me with a warm motherly touch
You shouted at me with tears in your eyes
You ignored people who said you were too soft

I remember you in the church choir
I remember you on the usher board

I remember you teaching Sunday school
I remember you taking communion
I know you prayed for us at the altar.

We did not come from a father-less home.
My people came from a mother-more home.
God could not be everywhere at once.
So He decided to make you mama.
The Creator knew that you could lead us.

You don't have to have a child to be "Mom"
You don't have to give birth to be "Mother"
You have carried enough to be " Mama"
You have labored enough to be "Mommy"
Your nurturing spirit has touched the world

There is no need for you to have a "day"
Your existence is far greater than that.
If I must take a "day" out of the year
To illustrate all that you mean to me
I'll wrap you up inside of my body
For nine months while your love pulses my soul.

11

Emancipated by God; Shackled by Tradition

It is not our mission to see through each other; it is our mission to see each other through.

Warning!!!! Reading this chapter will be hazardous to your bad health, for it will cause you to re-think your position on your so-called religion. Religion, as we know it, has become a fad; spirituality, however, is a focus. Religion is now our outward appearance, the face and demeanor we put on to impress others. Regardless of your faith, religion will shackle you in a tangled web of ignorance. For example, how many times have you heard ministers or parishioners use a Biblical reference only to discover the reference, quote or "ghost scripture" is nowhere in the Bible. This is, however, a traditional practice, one that we pass down from generation to generation, in the name of showing reverence to God. In essence though, we are only bastardizing His holy name because we fail to study and show ourselves worthy of His blessings.

First Sunday was genuinely sacred in my grandmother's home. We had to go to church on first Sunday. Not that other Sundays were insignificant, but first Sunday was "The" Sunday for communion. We'd all get up early to the smell of farm fresh eggs, bacon that must have come from "The Three Little Pigs" themselves, and pancakes that melted in your mouth like cotton candy. After the family breakfast, we all dressed to impress, led by Mama Ginia, with her colorful hats.

Church was always the same, except for the first Sunday. Somehow the ushers were more cordial, the choir more upbeat, and the Preacher more vocal and energetic on Communion Sunday. Still, the service was scripted and everyone played his or her part down to a tee!!!! Children were rarely taught about the genuine significance of communion, but we loved the cardboard bread and warm feeling the wine left in our bodies. We served God for two or three hours on Sunday and then went home for the Sunday feast of fried chicken, collard greens, pigs feet, yams, macaroni and cheese, rolls, peach cobbler and lemonade – HALELLUJAH!!!!!

By the way, the above description was not just my church through the years, but thousands of churches and denominations all across America – Shackled by tradition, loving, caring people who we call family and friends, all practicing the fad of religion instead of the focus of spirituality.

In the fad of religion, the youth have no real power. Many say the youth will operate the church in the future, but how can they be prepared when we use the church as a political power structure to oppress, depress, suppress and repress each other. In the midst of the confusion, our youth are leaving the church in droves. Sure, they are given ornamental "Youth Sundays," complete with youth choirs, readings and a speaker, but they are rarely or never allowed in on the decision making endeavors!!!! If we don't give our youth more meaningful roles, the streets will. The youth need more than a sprinkle of religion!! They need youth workshops with facilitators who know the language of the youth. The example of Jesus keenly illustrates the following: You can't teach them if you don't reach them!!!! Sex, drugs, alcohol, peer pressure, violence, profane music, language, etc. should all be discussed in church. If not there, Where?

It's time to transform the tradition that we've allowed to fester. We must learn and be reprogrammed! We must be willing to let God use us in order to uplift each other. We must leave our watches at home, and come to church ready to praise and worship His Holy Omnipotent name! The Shackles of "Sophisticated religion" must be replaced by "sincere Spirituality." How many times have you gone to church a little cracked, only to leave totally broken? It's time to spread more of the gospel and less of the gossip. Either you are in a crisis, you just left one or you are headed towards one. You deserve to dwell in a spiritual place where peace of mind in Christ is the top priority.

In spite of the churches that are sincere spiritual havens of warmth, we still have too many that are hell bent on preserving all traditions. When it comes to your soul and your sanity, do not let family and friends tell you to stay in the tenets of tradition. You deserve God's emancipation. If you just don't want to hurt anyone's feelings by changing your membership, keep your name on the roll, support the benevolent activities of the church and by all means, add a spark to the traditional, scripted service. Whatever you do, however, visit other churches to re-fuel. People will talk about you and slander your name, but you will in essence be moving closer to Christ. At this moment, I dare you to examine your spiritual walk and decide if you are shackled or free.

Thought: As an heir to God's kingdom here on earth and beyond, I will embrace my cross and my crown, even if it means going to church way across town! I deserve to be delivered!

First Aid Kit

Extra! Extra! Read all about it!
Satan is running wild
Snatching every man, woman and child
And we fall because of his charm and wit
Injuring each other, our supposed sisters and brothers
Does anyone have a First Aid Kit?

You may appear to be broke – but you don't have to be
 broken
You may be in the minority, but you don't have to be a token
Don't scratch if you don't itch
And don't bow down and sit
The church needs aid
Does anyone have a kit?

We blame the youth
But we failed to tell them the truth!
"Don't do as I do, do as I say," was our creed
Now our children choose the world because we don't have
what they need
Acting perfect as if we were the ones who had to hang and
bleed!
They aren't classy.
Their music is nasty and they're always jokin
Well many of us are skinnin and grinnin
And didn't you dance
When Clarence Carter sang "Strokin."

How many of us have sought the eye of a sister or brother
When we chose to wear a certain outfit?
Pray for one another. The pastor needs your aid
Does anyone have a first aid kit?

Organizations bickering,
Satan snickering,
Ushers (bored)-
"I can't praise the Lord."
Choirs singing a note,
But, you can't hear it,
If it's not inspired by the Holy Spirit.
Preacher preaching and you only say amen.
When it exposes someone else's sin,
But not your friend's
And you think your heart is gonna mend!
And the sincere ones are ready to quit,
But hold fast.
Your brother needs your aid,
Does anyone have a first aid kit?

I certainly can't judge
Cause there was a time Satan sat on my lap and I wouldn't
make him budge.
Now people see some of my glory
And they see some of your glory,
But they don't know our story!
They see our progress,
But they don't know our process!
And Satan tried to make us choke on his spit,
But Jesus gave us mouth to mouth,
So we could aid our sisters,

Does anyone have a first aid kit?

We have all been hurt, slandered and scarred
And from success, it appears as if we've been barred!
And the enemy has come with smiles on faces
In our family, social circles, churches and several races!
The enemy has prepared a mighty pit,
But Jesus has prepared a place in the presence of our
enemies where we can come and sit.
Spiritual, Economic, Social, Intellectual Freedom, we can
have all of it,
But we must possess faith, love, forgiveness and strength as
the utensils in our first aid kit!

You don't need the Red Cross to get your kit of first aid.
Just remember He died on the cross so your debt has already
been paid!!!!!!!!!

(KINDER) GARTEN

Aspire to be a vessel of love and light.
Believe in God and His purpose for you.
Care for the elderly and young.
Dedicate your life to service and greatness.
Envision your vision and exercise your right to exercise.
Forget about the past (live for your gift, the present).
Give to those less fortunate.
Humble yourself with honor not humiliation.
I am somebody (say this daily).
Joke around at least once a day.
Keep the faith, regardless of the circumstances.
Love everyone (even those who seemingly don't deserve it).

Make each day an adventure.
Never allow negative to nurture you.
Open your mind to creative thoughts.
Promise yourself peace of mind.
Quit putting yourself down.
Respect everyone's right to be………..
Smile! Smile! Smile! And Smile some more!
Touch with tender loving care.
Uplift the people and God will uplift you.
Vigorously exclaim your presence in life.
Work on your destiny!
X-ray your own heart first.
Yearn to learn.
Zestfully seek to complete meaningful tasks.
We teach our children their ABC's; now we must re-learn
ours.

12
Re-Tire or Retire

It is not our mission to see through each other; it is our mission to see each other through.

Re-Tire

You worked for someone called "Boss," "Supervisor,"
"Employer" or quite possibly "Sire."
And the company gave you a plaque because it was time for
 you to retire!

You labored long hours building someone else's empire,
And they gave you a little bonus when you decided to retire!

You always made ends meet as you placed cold food on the
fire,
And the job gave you a banquet once you decided to retire.

You got your social – insecurity coming, someone is a liar
You lived way below your means when you decided to
retire.

You chose to waste your money impressing others –
 materialism was your desire
 You did not invest wisely, so now it's almost impossible to
  retire.

You told your children and they are telling theirs – "Go find
 a good job and get hired
And because they didn't start their own businesses, when
downsized or fired
Your cycle starts again and you sincerely – Re-tire!!!!!!!

It's a tragic fact and a societal sin, But many who retired are
now working and getting tired all over again!

The tragedy is fact reader. My maternal grandmother is 82
years of age, and she still has to work, just to make ends meet!
She has given her time, talents, finances and heart to so many in
our family, yet no one is in a position to see that she retires;
instead, she has had to re-tire, living her last years out of the
realm of financial peace of mind. Sure, there are those who
desire to free "Mama Ginia" from her financial struggles, but no
one is in a position to. Even though much of the spending above
her means was her own doing, she deserves that financial peace
of mind because she has sacrificed so much for so many,
especially her children and grandchildren. "Mama Ginia's"
plight has motivated me to seek financial independence and
freedom. When I retire, prayerfully by 45, not 65, 75 etc., I
want my financial status to be the least of my worries.

Growing up and even today, I've heard the following quote-
countless times: Money is the root of all evil. I have discovered,
however, having no money is a powerful root of evil within
itself. I hear people proudly exclaim, "Money isn't everything"
or "I don't want to be rich, just comfortable." These sound so
admirable and well meaning, but the hardcore truth is often
excruciatingly painful to swallow: Without money, you cannot
achieve the so-called American dream. Without money, you
cannot pay your tithe in your chosen spiritual setting (which

should be <u>the</u> top priority). Without money, you cannot do any of the following:

(A)   Pay your tithes

(B)   Save

(C)   Invest

(D)   Pay Bills

(E)   Take a vacation

(F)   Have an evening of entertainment

(G)   Purchase a home

(H)   Purchase a dependable vehicle

(I)   Purchase clothing

(J)   Purchase food

(K)   Pay your children an allowance (they should learn the value of work now!)

(L)   Pay yourself

(M)   PAY YOUR TITHES!!!!!!

This is a brief list, and all of the above require money. In my family and many of yours, the cycle of poverty has been passed down from generation to generation. Many physical, emotional and psychological problems stem from a lack of saving and investing money wisely. The cycle of poverty has to stop somewhere, and I will die trying to be the interruption in the bloodline of family poverty. The so-called middle-class seems to be a form of poverty too. As I read my Bible, I study several scriptures that speak of the <u>love</u> of money as well as gaining wealth through dishonesty. The problem lies within the teaching. Many of us have been taught that wealth is wrong; we should have been taught, however, that greed is wrong, but benevolence is right. Many of us don't acquire blessings because we keep our little wealth bottled up and hidden. Surely no one can get in the bottle to be blessed by us, but God is also shut out of the bottle. The re-education process must now begin, and I will now give you a brief crash course on Money Management, one that will help you and future generations retire in happiness and prosperity not re-tire in misery and poverty.

(1)   Pay God First – No matter what you are told by family members, friends, the media, advertisers or others, give God 10% of your gross income. He gave you 100%, and He expects you to give 10% for the enhancement of his kingdom on earth and beyond. The government does not trust you to pay, so it takes 28-33% of your income. God takes nothing. He only gives. It is well documented that the Rockefellers, Getty's, Carnegie's and other prosperous individuals gave God 10% of their income and more. Presently, I am not financially independent. I pay God, and He always rewards me, on time, in time and most important during his time. Because of tithing, God has touched the hearts of others, and I've been blessed to have shelter, a vehicle, and other necessities of life while He blesses my business so all things will be in my name because I first pay and give honor to His name. Try giving Him 10% for three pay periods, and the calm and peace you receive in the midst of the storm will convince you to pay your tithes on a consistent basis.

(2)   Save your money and invest – Depending on your financial situation, you should always seek to save, save, save and invest, invest and invest. Stop allowing the cycle of "Living above our means" to destroy you. There are many investment strategies. Do the research; talk to financial analysts, and pray before making financial decisions. Teach your children to save. If their allowance runs out, don't continue to give, give,

give. Your employer does not give you bonuses because your money runs out. The more you invest and save, the less you regress and slave.

(3)   Stop Spending Money You Don't Have, Buying Things You Don't Need, To Impress People Who Don't Care About You- Many times, we buy in order to keep up with individuals who don't really care about our well-being. We attempt to buy children's love. We attempt to buy happiness. Money will not buy happiness. It should be used as a tool to build not destroy. P.T. Barnum once said, "There's a sucker born every minute." Don't be the sucker around the clock. You deserve to have some luxuries in life, but don't allow the luxuries to supercede the priorities. If you must have name brand clothing, be an intelligent consumer and purchase the items from the store that offers the most economical price. Furthermore, when your children are forced into the name brand lifestyle by you, don't be surprised when they place materialism above financial independence. Don't be shocked if you can't afford these expensive items one day, and our daughters prostitute themselves or our sons sell drugs in the name of fashion. There is nothing wrong with name brands, but let your children know their name is just as important as any on their behinds. The behind can never have more value than the mind!!! If it does, your children will be left behind in the future. I'm not an analyst, but I have analyzed and witnessed people living a six-figure lifestyle on a four or five figure income. Don't just spend the money, grow it. As my parents used to say, "Don't let a dollar burn your pockets." If you added all expenses at the end of the month, I'm almost certain you'd discover an extra $100.00 or more could have been saved or

invested. If there's too much month left at the end of the money, you seriously need to examine your spending habits!

(4)   Give back to the Community – Benevolence is admirable. You may not be able to give millions to education like Bill Cosby, Bill Gates or Oprah Winfrey, but you can give some of the wasted cash to charity or sponsor a child in your neighborhood or church who is in need. Give to a family member, friend, or complete stranger who is down and out. Or simply give because it feels so good to see others light up with joy. Remember: we make our living by what we get; we make our lives by what we give. When you free up blessings, God will bless you with an abundance of what you want, need and deserve.

(5)   Be a gift owner not gift loaner – It's time to stop allowing others to make money off of your gift. You have to be a gift owner, one who will step out on faith, combine that faith with works and inspire. Your Just Over Broke is not enough. You don't deserve to live from paycheck to paycheck. Sit down, map out a plan and market your gift. You don't need an abundance of training. God has already ordained you to give your gift ownership, and through ownership, you can motivate the masses! Whether it's singing, baking, building, public speaking, invest in your gift. There is nothing wrong with having more income when the outcome of your false income is not sufficient! As a nation, we are always concerned with civil rights. That's fine, but we also need to focus on our silver rights. Your gift is calling you; it wants to be unlocked and given the freedom to run wild!

Regardless of the circumstance, I am going to continue to promote my gift. I am not obsessed with or by money. I'm tired of seeing poverty and despair. I'm tired of the cycle of poverty. I'm sick and tired of being sick and tired! A good friend and co-consultant of mine, Furman Gatewood, Jr. told me: 9 to 5 until we're 65-95 is not an option. Reader, at this moment I dare you to stop allowing the media romance to destroy your finances. Don't depend on the government or your employer. Get your financial house in order right now. Future generations will thank you for it in your absence, and the present ones will salute you now!

Thought: When the time comes, I will retire not re-tire. I will embrace and gain my silver rights!

13
If It Runs In The Family, Chase It Out Now!!!!!

It is not our mission to see through each other; it is our mission to see each other through.

I must begin this chapter by being blunt: **ALL RELATIVES AIN'T FAMILY!!!** The "ain't," an informal substitute for "are not," is needed here because there's nothing standard, proper or correct about the misguided negativity made appropriate due to the ultimate statement of ignorance: **IT RUNS IN THE FAMILY!!!** Often, the ancestors have allowed it to fester; the descendents were not repentant, so now the seeds are forced to bleed!!!! When it comes to "running in the family," we must pass the baton to the following:

1.	Fear of God
2.	Love
3.	Peace of Mind
4.	Unity
5.	Intellectual Pursuits
6.	High Expectations
7.	Economic Growth
8.	Family Reunions
9.	Respect for the elderly
10.	A vision for the youth

These are just 10, and I chose them because of the Ten commandments, W.E.B. Dubois reference to the talented tenth and my flight from Charlotte to Savannah is scheduled to arrive at 10:00p.m. I just completed a speech at the University of Tennessee, and my breakfast with Dr. Ronald McFadden, Director of the Ronald McNair Scholars Program was at 10:00a.m. Furthermore, we often measure the quality of someone or something using a scale of one to ten!!!

Generation after generation in many families has suffered because generations from before have allowed the negative traditions to fester like a sore that even Job would detest. In my poem Generation X to Generation EXCELLENT, an exclaimer says the following:

It appears as if the world has become a victim of a cruel hex.
Everything negative is now blamed on Generation X.
But remember, Generation X learns from the examples
Being set by the generations before X!!!!

We need only look in the mirror to discover why our youth often appear out of control.

I get so tired of hearing people say, "His dad was like that or her mom was just as negative." We must not promote negative behavior in the name of, "It runs in the family." If Granddaddy was abusive and Daddy was abusive, we should not stand by and wait for sons to be abusive. The abusive men ought to be the ones to inform the sons that abuse isn't acceptable; however, this is not a perfect world! Someone with God in their life, courage and compassion must step forward and attempt to train those sons in a different manner. I know it's not easy, but watching mothers, wives, aunts, daughters, and nieces suffer is far worse than stepping forward to break the cycle of abuse. I firmly believe that any man who physically or emotionally abuses women is not fit to have a woman placed in his existence.

Also, if Grandma was tolerant of beatings and mama was tolerant, we should train daughters to recognize the signs of abuse. In families of all races and cultures, women are groomed to be weak, dependent vessels of inferiority. This is not the will of God. It is the will of the ignorance that has been in families across America for decades. I'm not suggesting that women be rebels. They shouldn't have to be. They need to be viewed as the jewels that produce our most precious gifts, our children. Too often, Men and Women are at odds because their parents were at odds and their parents and so on!!!

In all families, we must stop "playing church." This "Sunday dress rehearsal" mentality has been running in our families for years. There will be no sincere family healing until there is a sincere family fear of God. Even as adults, we must be childlike in the presence of God. He doesn't want our ornamental religion. He wants steadfast spirituality. If there seems to be an abundance of suffering and lack of healing in your family, trace your roots and see what has been allowed to, "Run in the family." I know I need to pray more, and seek deliverance from Him, not cousin so and so. Until we develop personal relationships with God, peace of mind will be an unreachable afterthought. It's time for your family to run to God!!!

High expectations, intellectual pursuits and economic growth must be allowed to, "Run in the family." If you live in a family where "average" has been acceptable, you need to spend time in a family where "excellence" is the standard, hoping that your example will rub off on others. Caution: You will be ostracized by relatives, but remember, "All relatives ain't family." Sincere family members, even those reluctant to join you, will not degrade you. If you have a desire to be great but fear family ridicule, you must remember that God has a plan for each of us, and you may be the chosen emancipator for future generations. If you fail, the cycle of mediocrity will continue.

Now, more than ever, we must genuinely encourage the youth of our family to have super-vision. We need to encourage them to exemplify Philippians 4:13: *I can do all things through Christ who strengthens me.* I get angry when I hear spiritual leaders or family members say, "You don't need an education – all you need is Jesus." Christ Himself promoted wisdom. We need only to remind our youth to be humble, honorable and benevolent once they attain an education. We must encourage our family members to seek spiritual, intellectual, cultural and economic freedom.

The following list is a sincere contrast to the first one outlined in this chapter. It illustrates those things that should be chased out of our families:

1.   Fake Religion (Playing Church)
2.   Hatred
3.   Abuse
4.   Drug and alcohol usage
5.   Mediocrity Lack of discipline
6.   (children at the head of households)
7.   Ignoring the elderly
8.   Jealousy
9.   Ignoring emotional & psychological wounds that damage us for life.
10.   Acceptance of JOBs (Just Over Broke) instead of careers

These are just ten, but there are so many more. It is time to embrace the positive in our families with pride. We are human, so mistakes are inevitable. It is tragic, however, when we don't seek to learn from our mistakes. It is time to communicate more and gossip less.

Reader, there is an issue in your family that you desire to address. What's stopping you? Examine your heart. Go to someone in the family you trust and vibe with. Make certain, however, that family member is a beacon of light and not confusion. You must now step forward and set an example that will appear strange to some and downright crazy to others. Just remember, you were made in the image of your Heavenly Father before you were given your family name. Put on your spiritual sneakers and prepare to run it out!!!

At this very moment, I dare you to sit at the head of the table, conquering the negative that your family has digested and feasted upon for years!

Thought: In order for my family to fly, I cannot allow the negative to run!!!

14
Tongue Twister

"It is not our mission to see through each other; it is our mission to see each other through."

Person #1:	Yo man, pass me the grub so I can get my eat on!!!
Person #2:	Slide dat dere bowl ovah here!
Person #3:	Excuse me, would you mind passing the meat and vegetables to me?

The three examples of language all convey the same message, but only one can be used on a universal scale, the third one. All three can be used, depending on the environment you're in, but only the third one will be slated as Standard American English. Standard American English is known as formal language, and many describe it as "proper." The first two examples are known as informal and/or slang. This chapter will examine several types of language, and illustrate why formal language is the best to know as well as the best to use.

Language of the Family

In many instances the success or failure of an individual begins in his/her family. Language is a major part of this. Parents, guardians, and others in the family should practice using formal language in front of their children and other children in the family. Although informal language or slang is commonly used in our homes, it does not mean that society will embrace our family language customs. Slang will not be the language in school, and children who are taught to speak correct English will have an advantage over those who are not. Growing up and even today, I've heard the following: "Keith, you talk proper like them white folks." Every time I do a speech, conduct a workshop or facilitate a symposium, I always come in contact with individuals who have heard the same nonsense. Not surprising, most of them are successful in their careers and all have said language played a major role in their success. I've often wondered: If talking correctly is white, what is the label for talking black? Don't ridicule members of your family if they desire to use formal language. Furthermore, if you do use formal language and your use of it came about through formal educational training, don't look down on those who choose not to use it or haven't had formal training. For instance, my grandparents and other elders always spoke informal language, but it was universal for them and to them. Moreover, our elders did not have the opportunities for empowerment that we enjoy today. Our elders paved the way for us, and we stand on their shoulders. Quite often, the immediate descendents of slaves were physically, emotionally, and mentally brutalized if they even thought about advancing themselves, especially academically and economically.

The language of the family is used daily. It is popular at the dinner table and family reunions or other gatherings. The danger, however, is if children only embrace the slang or informal use of language, these children grow up with the informal as their guide. Even when trained in school, they'll often feel the need to "fit in" or be accepted. The New Millennium will require most of its successful people to be able to speak formally. Those who won't face such a requirement will be in Sports and Entertainment. This does not mean, however, that athletes and entertainers are not well spoken; it only means that their talent supercedes their conversation, depending on their career choice. Don't be ashamed to enhance the language of the family.

Language of the Streets/Community

This area is probably the most flexible. Many times, it's where we are most comfortable. We may attempt to keep a certain image around others, but with peers we can let our guards down. The language of the streets is not racial in nature. It's human in nature. There are terms of informal language that are universally used to communicate. For example, in Black and White communities, a person acting crazy is described as "tripping." In many Hispanic communities, this person is called "loco" (wild). Furthermore, in the Black community, when a person is perceived as one assimilating or trying to be white, he or she is labeled a "sell out," "Uncle Tom" or "Oreo." In the Native American community, this same individual is described as an "Apple." I cannot speak for the actions of those who are characterized, but if the criteria for being called "Oreo" or "Apple" is usage of Standard American English, then both are invalid. The language of the community, while valid at times, is not a prerequisite for success. Standard American English needs to be used, even if not mastered. The community should encourage its members to be more versatile. The language of the streets will, for the most part, keep people on the lower end of the economic bracket in America. People should not be ashamed when using informal language at times, but they need to know when and where to use it.

The following list is an example of appropriate language venues.

Formal	Informal/Slang
1. Classroom	1. Cafeteria
2. Career	2. JOB (Just Over Broke)
3. Career Interview	3. Athletic event, movie, concert etc.
4. Banquet	4. Fast Food Restaurant
5. Bank	5. Family Reunions (informal setting)
6. Family Reunions (formal setting)	
7. All the time!!!	

I refuse to apologize for using the language of success. Moreover, I must caution my readers: It is quite difficult to turn language on and off. Language is not a television set or radio. People will define you through your use of language. Whether right or wrong, just or unjust, the overwhelming majority of successful Americans are those who can master formal language. In the following scenario, which doctor would you go to?

(A)   Yo, your heart be all messed up!!!

(B)   Excuse me; there are serious problems with your heartbeat.

You can substitute professions and scenarios, and I'm almost certain you would spend your hard earned money with those who sounded like business people. The choice is yours reader.

At this very moment, I dare you to embrace Standard American English, not as a temporary buddy but as a lifelong friend.

Thought: I won't use formal English just for show. I'll make it a part of me, so I can continue to grow.

15
Spare the Rod, Spoil the Nation

It is not our mission to see through each other; it is our mission to see each other through.

I was so ashamed: everyday I had to leave my "homeboys" (friends) and "fly girls" (young ladies) and report to the house when the street lights came on; never mind the fact most of the action took place when the sun went down; still, I had to be at 178-29 147th Avenue Jamaica Queens, New York or suffer the wrath of my parents. This was the ritual for fall, winter, and spring during the early to mid 80's; during summers at 1523 and 1524 Arcadian Street Savannah, Georgia, the same consistency was in tact. My grandparents and an uncle and aunt became surrogate parents, and when the streetlights came on, I went in. Sure I was ridiculed, called such names as "Cindefella" and "Earlybird," but my peers' laughter was nothing compared to a New York City belt or a Georgia switch; it appeared as if no one in my family advocated sparing the rod. Even my older siblings verbally disciplined me when I got out of line; this was in order because quite often-older siblings were the caretakers of younger ones, especially in the streets and extended community. My cousins, neighboring playmates and I ("Da Fellas," as we were called) knew the deal. We either obeyed our elders or heard the following exhalations: "Go get me a switch, you are grounded for two weeks, shut up before I give you something to cry for, Oh, so now you're grown, etc. etc..."

These were indeed my years of early adolescence, a time of hormonal growth and discoveries. It was also the last era of respect for the elders, discipline and tough love. Many opponents and special interest groups call discipline abuse, but that so called abuse saved thousands of my peers nationwide. Yet the generation after us (the 80's) has suffered and is dying physically and emotionally due to a lack of discipline and a systematic lynching of youth of all races and socio-economic backgrounds.

The 90's and New Millennium have birthed a new idea of "passive parenting." As a teenager (13-16) I had to obey the wishes of my parents. At 17, I was able to live with my aunt Daisy and twin cousins Kenny and Kelvin because my parents moved south. Kenny and Kelvin protected me, and my parents' example and discipline kept me out of trouble. There was no compromise unless a special community event was taking place or I was at a friend's home, which had adult supervision in place. During the 90's, however, and especially today, children who haven't even reached the age of 10 are wandering hopelessly in drug and violence infested streets and society nationwide is in a zombie like stupor concerning this travesty!!! Today, thousands of teens are raising their parents and have become the heads of households. As I do speeches and seminars across the nation, I hear parents say, "I can do nothing with her/him." This is indeed a tragic state of affairs. When our children are allowed to make parental decisions, what happens to us? We become victims of the system.

System Often Says: <u>Reason With the Child</u>

The "system" here is defined as any entity (media, family, schools, governmental agencies, etc.) that implores parents to place their children on an equal level. I often hear several talk show hosts say, "We must reason with our children." That's the <u>reason</u> we're in this sad predicament today. The "system" tells us to make our children feel equal. The idea is so "cute" and "nice," but not realistic. Had I thought I was my parent's equal, I would have stayed out way past my assigned curfew. Had I thought I was my parent's equal, some of that innate respect would have dwindled away. The same "system" that tells parents not to discipline their children is the same one that is pumping more funds into prisons than into schools. It's the same system that ignored the cries of parents in Littleton, Colorado before the Columbine massacre. Had the "system" investigated the unusual behavior of Eric Harris and Dylan Klebold, perhaps that tragedy would have never reaped its poisonous head upon American soil. That same "system" has us believing that only certain types of teenagers commit crimes. We listen to "system says" more than we listen to "Simon Says," and Simon was sincere and unbiased. Don't be hoodwinked by any part of the "system." Your children need discipline and tough love. I refuse to allow the "system" to raise my son, "son by spirit, not sperm." He has no idea of the stereotypes and negative propaganda. My nieces, nephews, surrogate children who I work with through several foundations and school systems nationwide have no clue as to the statistics, but I do!!!!!! I abhor child abuse, but I'm not a fan of children abusing parents either. The sincere love must replace the "system's" idea of animated love.

Start in the Womb

Saving our children in anticipation of being productive citizens begins early. It means reprogramming what we are, who we are and whose we are. It means, "Don't do as I do, do as I say do" will be deemed invalid. Straight out of the womb, babies will mimic sounds, patterns and behaviors. We must be models for our children and each other. Children are usually innocent. We are often the opposite. We must teach our children respect, tact and character through our actions, not just words but actions. I recall a simple phrase I heard my junior high school assistant principal, Mr. Smith, say: "Keith, I'd rather see a sermon than hear one." This was a simple phrase, but one I've respected and had to repeat because of my past transgressions. When we seek to "raise" our children, we must do just that. We must elevate them to a level pleasing in God's sight, not the sight of others. We cannot allow them to be adults as children and expect them to be obedient at our beck and call. I've often heard of the 5 year old who is allowed to use profanity because it's "cute," and when he/she becomes 15, he/she is beating his/her parents, is in juvenile detention or even worse, DEAD!!!! There is no magical formula for rearing children, but the Biblical text of Ephesians 6: states, " Raise them in the nurture and admonition of the lord." In order for us to do so, we must first be willing to submit to God. Reader, there are times when we raise our children with diligence, discipline and love, and they still go astray. What will happen if we don't raise them with diligence, discipline and love? We must give them genuine love that will take them from the womb until they reach the

tomb!!! If we continue to spare the rod (discipline not abuse),
we will certainly spoil our children and our nation.

At this very moment, I dare you to become the nurturing
parent or surrogate parent you were created to be, for if you
don't step forward, the streets will take your children and your
family backward.

*Thought: I will communicate with my children as a <u>leader</u>,
not a <u>breeder</u>. I will discipline, not <u>abuse</u>; as a family we will
win, not <u>lose</u> – I will be the head of my family and God will be
the head of us all!!!*

King of the Cast (II)

Dedicated to Charles E. Jordan – my father by spirit, not
sperm – the one whose voice made me harken and whose heart
made me honorable, my other fathers, biological and surrogate,
my son Keon Jamal, and all of my nephews.

The statistics are wrong
because they place you in the
Race of life, dead <u>last</u> –

But you taught me how to run with honor and you
Are a mighty King of the <u>Cast</u>.

I cried in your arms when thinking of the <u>past</u> –
And you held me with Patriarchal Promise –
You mighty King of the <u>Cast</u>!

Even when I thought I was grown with disrespect
Rolling off my tongue and other negative <u>trash</u> –

You scolded me, gently spanked me, and soothed me
because
You were the King of the <u>Cast</u>.

Life is indeed a play and we should seek to perform
Our parts with dignity and <u>class</u> –
I've learned from your examples and now
I'm crowned as a King of the <u>Cast</u>.

To fathers in small towns and big <u>cities</u> seeking to
Find common ground with sons in <u>unity</u> –
It takes a crown of "example" to be the
King of the Cast, where the (LE) stands for
Living Eternally!!!!!

Let your spirit be greater than your sperm!!!!!

From the Womb to the Tomb
A Sequel to "Mother More"

Dedicated to the women of my family and mothers'
nationwide

I am so blessed you made room in the womb
Your God given gentle touch has kept me from the tomb!
I still remember (as a child) the scent of your perfume
I know you'll be with me from the womb to the tomb.

Lady you were so fine, even with your scarf, mop and
broom,

I know that you'll be with me from the womb to the tomb.
Even during those spankings after I had given my teachers
doom...
I knew you'd be with me from the womb to the tomb.

"Get ready for Sunday school; boy clean your room!"
 Your voice burns in my heart from the womb to the tomb.
 I came out of one womb, but I've had several mothers
 I love you "Mother More" and thank Jehovah for all the
 others.

Mother, Mommie, Mama, Mom – all do sincerely apply
God creates his vessels, so I don't ask why
Because of your strength, in life I'll always try
God asked me what I thought of you and this was my reply:
    She's my favorite lady, has been all my life
    I hope her strength is in the Queen I'll one day
    Choose as my wife
Thank you Lord for Mother's; when judgement day
Comes and you send the apocalyptic boom-
I know I can't hide in her womb-
But if I am faithful, I'll ascend from my tomb
Into your heavenly room.

16
Dream Walking

It is not our mission to see through each other; it is our mission to see each other through.

During the past twelve months, I've appeared on the Oprah show as a motivational guru. I've donated millions of dollars to the church, charity and Savannah State University. I've delivered speeches on a national and international level. My children were leaders in most aspects of life, and my wife and I were a dynamic duo, inspiring thousands through speeches and songs. CHITLINS was a #1 best seller, and other self-help books were being manifested. Life was truly worth living, not surviving. These and other divine thoughts were born out of one of my favorite past times, WALKING!!! Yes walking. When I want to release a great deal of stress, I usually jog, engage in some other sporting event, or do push-ups, but when I want to exercise in excellence, I walk, walk, and walk some more. In the year 2000-2001, I dreamed the impossible while walking alone. Dream walking is so fulfilling because it's just you and nature, not the chaos of civilization. The following steps will guide you in turning your dream – walking into visions which come to fruition:

Walk in an environment of Peace

In order to dream without constant interruption, don't walk in heavy populated areas. Too many fellow walkers can be a distraction. Quite often, you will wind up paying attention to others and not your dreams. I love walking at Lake Mayer in Savannah, Georgia. Its 1 ½ mile circular design, highlighted by calming waters and ducks is so serene and soothing to my soul. I'm able to walk and dream in a 360-degree of peace. I choose to walk when the track has very little traffic. While walking in this environment of peace (usually for one hour or 4 ½ miles), I go on joyous journeys that only enhance my thirst to succeed. You must walk in a place or an area that isn't too loud with music, traffic or people. The key is thoroughly immersing yourself within yourself and taking you to a new level of greatness through your dreams. One word of caution: Be aware of your surroundings and those in your surroundings. With crime at an all-time high, we can never be too careful. I don't want dream walking to be a nightmare of stalking.

Walk with soothing, soft music

During your dream walk, I would not advise you to listen to any loud music, whether it be classical, heavy metal, rap, rock, country, R&B, jazz or gospel. You may listen to the soothing sounds in this category, but avoid too much base or high-powered instruments and solos. Many stores sell "Nature Music," or music, which is calming to the mind and soul. The music you choose must merge with your mind to enhance your dreams, not your emotions or ability to dance or sing along. The music should become the theme music of the dream. I choose no music because it is distracting to my dreams. Sounds such as birds chirping or waves gently splashing on the rocks are soothing. The bottom line is this: If you must wear those headphones, listen to the music that keeps you focused on the dream and not the beat or lyrics to a song.

Walk Alone

Walking and/or workouts are very inspiring in our quest to complete our self-imposed goals of physical fitness. I love doing Tae-Bo with my fiancé, jogging with relatives or friends while we verbally push each other to victory, or competing against individuals in a basketball game. All of these are wonderful. However, when I want to dream and still get the benefits of being active through exercise, I walk alone. When you walk alone, you become the CEO of the company, head of the law firm, master educator, polished-public speaker, star student or vibrant volunteer. When you dream walk alone, you feel a mighty rush of power because it's just you, God and nature. When you walk alone, God can speak greatness in you and you will listen because there will be no one else to listen to. When you walk alone, your focus will be greater and your dreams will turn into the aforementioned vision.

At this point, you may be saying, "What is a dream and what is a vision?" The dream, reader, is what you are able to see in your mind, often with physical eyes only. The vision is the manifestation of the steps of how to make those dreams come true, and the vision takes more than just physical eyes. You must use the symbolic eyes of the spirit and the soul. In May of 1999, I took a long dream walk in a beautiful rural town in Georgia called Dublin. It was not just the luck of the Irish around me. It was the omnipresent nature of God showing me a portion of my destiny. I saw myself motivating people on national television. Reader, six months later, I appeared on "Showtime at the Apollo." Only God knew what was next. So I am now and will forever be a staunch dream walker. Join me and the dreams may just give birth to an odyssey of reality.

At this very moment, I dare you to put on soothing socks and sneakers and take a dream-walk. Not only will you prosper physically, your mind will get a welcome taste of sweet serenity.

Thought: I will diligently pursue dream walking until I wake up into greatness.

Young Souls Held at Bay:
Dedicated to the elders of my family and elders everywhere.

Only the elders know the <u>deal</u>
but the young think they know the way
because of their vigor and <u>zeal.</u>

They haven't felt what the elders <u>feel</u>
They haven't seen the dark of day
Only the elders know the <u>deal</u>.

Lips barely off the breast, legs just off the big <u>wheel</u>
They think they know what to say
because of their vigor and <u>zeal.</u>

They know not what is <u>real</u>
They life is one big play
Only the elders know the <u>deal</u>.

Greatness is in an envelope, but they can't break the <u>seal</u>
From the truth they are led astray
because of their vigor and <u>zeal.</u>

While on streets called Lenox, Auburn and <u>Beale</u>
Young souls are held at bay
 Only the elders know the <u>deal</u>
because of their vigor and <u>zeal</u>.

17
Exalt the Elders

It is not our mission to see through each other; it is our mission to see each other through.

In almost every family, there exists a patriarchal and/or matriarchal figure; society calls these people the elderly, aged, senior citizens or old people. They are, however, simply our roots to many oak trees of strength, endurance and compassion. They are the ones who tell epic adventures of walking ten miles in order to get to school to receive an education that we take for granted. The monologue is often universal and goes like this:

We didn't have all these luxuries of today. We didn't have televisions and cars and a lot of clothes. We wore hand – me – downs. We pumped water from the well and worked from sun – up to sun – down. We didn't disrespect our elders cause we knew we wouldn't be able to sit down for a while. We had pride and dignity and faith in God. We got along with one another and took care of one another. Everybody raised everybody's children, and we all ate. Y'all are so blessed today. You got everything but the sense you was born with. Lord have mercy!

That last part is the reason we are so blessed today. Our elders have prayed us through many hardships over the years. Grandparents are the manifestation of ultimate compassion. They often raise their children's children for various reasons. When parents are beckoned to exclaim, "NO" to our many requests, it is often the grandparents who exclaim, "YES." I don't advocate this difference of opinion, but I have often been the beneficiary of this actual/factual war of kinfolk.

Our first piece of candy, most delicious meal, best wardrobe and countless lessons on life all came from our grandparents. And when our parents got on our last nerves, we all ran and sat on granddaddy's lap or placed our heads in grandma's lap. They were always *"simply grand!"*

The "golden gems" of my family set the tone for my thirst for greatness. Mama Ginia made sure I had hot grits in my stomach and a relaxer in my royal kinky hair. Her smile always reassured me that I was a royal priesthood. Granddaddy Horace made sure I went to bed on time, did my indoor and outdoor chores, ate his famous bologna sandwiches, complete with his fingerprints planted deep in the fresh baked Sunbeam bread as a result of pressing too hard while cutting them in half. He also introduced me to the infamous "switch of the South," the grandparents favorite tool of discipline. Mama Lillie was such a jewel. She introduced wrestling, fried Mega hamburgers, sugarcane, sincere laughter and coffee. No one was allowed to say a negative word about me in her presence. When I visited her sister (my Aunt Rhoda – I said Rhody all my life), she'd always call just to see if her "Keithy" was fine. Mama Jordan got me hip to chocolate milk in Cheerios and cold chicken out of the shoebox while riding the train from Georgia to New York. She always made me perform for the other passengers. She was my agent and had no idea she was feeding my spirit of public speaking at such an early age. She's 90 years young and just purchased a new vehicle! Grandma Bertha Mae always greeted me with such a smile and her genuine, "How my baby." I recall being on a tour with a College Concert and she fed over 50 students. Ma Mildred gave me sweets until I couldn't eat anymore. That was my prize for rubbing her feet with sandpaper. She was a true nurturer during my childhood. Mama Reeves was the Rice Krispies Treat Queen, and Friday's at her house meant a trip to Vandy's Seafood restaurant. She always had a kind word, no matter what the circumstances were. To this day, she always sends me a love token. Daddy Reeves made sure he took the fellas on the back of the truck for a tour of the sawmills, swamps and scenes of Brooklet, Georgia. Aunt Cat was my greatest vocal supporter during my early days of speech delivery. She'd moan with a high pitched voice and shout Amen all the way to heaven. Uncle Ike told stories of beating Joe Louis and playing along side Jackie Robinson and Pee Wee Reese. Hyperbole was his middle name. Uncle Rufus and Mama Ella always had a house full of people and hearts of gold. Uncle Rufus was a hunter, so you never knew what you were gong to eat on any given night. Nana (Queen Bee) bought my graduation suit and sheltered all her grands.

There are so many more elders of inspiration in my family, and some on this list had "gone on home" (as the old folk like to say), but memories of them only enhance my thirst to succeed and give a little back of what so many of them have given to me.

They were all were different, but two things flowed off their lips with serious conviction: Fear and Serve God and get an education. Reader the names and situations are different in your family, but I'm sure you can relate. Everyone has an Uncle W. L., the old wise jokester who gives impromptu speeches. You must have an uncle Fulley; one who prays for a lifetime it seems. You know an Aunt Alfreida, one who beckons the youth to build a family empire. You must have a Grandma Hutchins, one who gives you a pair of socks or underwear every Christmas. The elders are works of art who deserve to be exalted, not above God – but surely above the rest of us.

The following is a small guide that you can use to elevate the elders:

(A).   Communicate with them often. The elders have an abundance of wisdom to share. They are walking, talking, and breathing history books. When communicating with them, be an active listener and allow their knowledge to take you to a level of greatness. One of the greatest gifts we can impart to the elderly is an ear. The stories they tell are more inspiring, humorous and triumphant than any television show or movie. Communication with the elderly adds life to them and meaning to our lives.

(B).   Video the elderly. Quite often we tell younger generations about their ancestors, but getting their stories on tape would be so much more effective. When the golden ones leave this earth, we could have more than just a memory and photos. We could have family documentaries. All it takes is a little time and effort. Family reunions and other gatherings would have greater significance because the voices of the elderly would always be present.

(C).   Help them financially if they cannot help themselves. It is the responsibility of the descendants of the grandparents to help them maintain financial stability. Some may ask why, yet it is quite simple. We must seek to give back to those who gave so much to us. Families must learn to pool resources together so that the elderly don't suffer financial hardships during their last years here on earth. One person can't do it all in a family, but those who benefited from the generosity of the elders can unite to do just a little. Walking a long journey begins with one step at a time. It is our duty to take care of those who nurtured us when we couldn't nurture ourselves. It is a divine responsibility of the descendants to provide as much financial peace of mind for the elderly as possible.

(D).   Don't allow their struggle to be in vain. We will all make mistakes and have ups and downs in life, but we must work steadfast to make the elders proud. I can recall attending a high school graduation and seeing a proud grandmother. She was in a wheelchair, but she got up and used a walker to get to her seat. Upon asking her why she was present, this 80 something woman of grace and greatness, one whose limbs were losing strength but not her soul – looked at me and proudly exclaimed, "I'm here to see my baby graduate." It seemed as if all her years of struggle and sacrifice were made whole in that one moment. We should all work and live in a way that makes the elders smile and cry with unceasing happiness. For them, it doesn't take much. They just want to know that we will be able to take care of ourselves.

Those are just a few, but they are vital for the preservation of precious legacies. At this moment, I dare you to call, write, or visit and elder, for they know the road and we must find our way!

Thought: I will utilize the sense I was born with.

18
Haiku Hype

It is not our mission to see through each other; it is our mission to see each other through.

Note: A haiku is a Japanese form of poetry; each poem has three lines and a total of 17 syllables, five in line one, seven in line two and five in line three.

I sincerely believe the Haiku is one of the most powerful forms of poetry. Provocative messages are given in a mere three lines and seventeen syllables. The following pages of Haiku, the shortest child in the poetry family will provide tall, bold, universal messages that will leave you in a state of literacy and literal shock. Everyday topics and traditions will be challenged and possibly changed as a result of three lines. Three, however, is a number of greatness. The Holy trinity is universally accepted as the epitomizing principle of spirituality. Furthermore, it is universally accepted that Christ's resurrection took place on the third day. "Three strikes and you're out" is used in baseball, America's game. The Three Little Pigs," "Goldie Locks and The Three Bears," and "Three Blind Mice" have thrilled children for decades. The Haiku is about to step forward and take its place in the realm of topics we discussed daily.

Religion is a fad; Spirituality is a focus
Denominations
are not ordained by the Lord
one line on judgement.

Don't blame the devil
for the hell that lies within
God won't accept that.

Please study the word
Sunday is not the Sabbath
show thyself approved.

Died on Calvary
for the sins of the whole world
just so we could live.

The youth are leaving
because they have no power
in the church today.

The bread is my source
the wine is my salvation
I hunger no more.

Is heaven your goal?
Don't create hell here on earth.
You will not ascend.

Satan comes in all
races, cultures and backgrounds
Universal sin!!!

Family Reunions

Telling many tales
the old folks exaggerate
the younger ones laugh.

The ribs are so good
the desserts are scrumptious too
ice cold lemonade!

T – shirts worn with pride
the ancestors are on front
the tree is on back.

Members from up North
tease the southern cousins speech
they sound so proper?

Playing games like spades
and hanging out on the town
cousins and siblings.

In historic sites
like Savannah and New York
kinfolk do gather.

Giving you titles
the elderly do it well
that's not my name ma'am.

We bless the living
we pay tribute to the dead
pray for the unborn.

Videos and slides
photo albums from the past
precious memories.

Church on Sunday morn
relatives sit together
then all do depart!

Looking Over Various Experiences (LOVE)

Was your heart broken
By someone you did love
Love yourself again

Why is it we
Often hurt those we love the most
Especially ourselves

You did fall in love
You lost your balance somehow
Next time you must stand

Brother Romeo
Fell in love with Juliet
I miss Verona!

Material things
Are not a part of true love
They do control lust!

Love me at first sight?
Do you really trust your eyes?
Infatuation!

The lust of the flesh
Will only build the body?
Make love to my mind!

A strong gentle hug
Is needed by all of us
OXYMORONIC

You can't cheat on me
If you study for the test

Love is an exam

Love Universal
All people need to be loved
The agape love!

We were genuine as children

Let's play hide and go
seek a better way to live
free from monkey bars.

Mama wiped the blood
from my infected kneecap
the alcohol burned.

I dropped my candy
and I kissed it up to God
to take away germs.

Afraid of the dark
The boogie man will get us
We did pee the bed!

We played games daily
We smelled like the great outdoors
We ran from the switch!

We hated to bathe
Splashed, water on our bodies
And dried off quickly

Opened all our toys
We played with them for a week
Closets became home

I said my short speech
In a brand new Easter suit
After the egg hunt

We fought everyday
Never became enemies
Adults should learn too!

I was promoted
I showed off my report card
My parents were proud.

AND ON THE 8TH DAY

Dedicated to all educators nationwide

AND ON THE 8TH DAY GOD CREATED
TEACHERS
To nurture the **MASSES** in their classes
He gave the ability to write and read
And pass it on to youth of all **CREEDS!**

AND ON THE 8TH DAY GOD CREATED
TEACHERS
Not to be underpaid or taken for **GRANTED**
But to water seeds that must be planted!
Lawyers, doctors, politicians, and preachers
All professionals were molded by teachers
He gave them the ability to write and read
And pass it on to youth of all **CREEDS**

AND ON THE 8TH DAY GOD CREATED
TEACHERS
Like the mother who carries her unborn child
And father who waits to see his image for nine months
Each year teachers carry the young
Help them to crawl, walk, run, and
fly towards success, never cutting
the symbolic surrogate umbilical cord.

AND ON THE 8TH DAY GOD CREATED
TEACHERS
He gave them the ability to write and read
And pass it on to youth of all CREEDS.
If professions were movies
Education would be the feature
If you can read this tribute
Then go and thank a TEACHER!

AND ON THE 8TH DAY...

19

And On the 8th Day...

It is not our mission to see through each other; it is our mission to see each other through.

It is my sincere prayer that once you complete this chapter, you'll have the greatest respect and admiration for the teachers of our great nation. Presently, Public education is under attack by many different facets of society. Teachers are being blamed for all that is negative in the academic lives of our children and youth, yet they are given little or no credit for the positive strides our children and youth are making. Certainly everyone who is employed has a major responsibility for the growth and stability of their profession. Teachers, however, labor in a profession where their influence and performance have a direct effect on the progression or regression of our nation's future leaders. Very few people in America can stake that claim. Educators are negatively, not constructively, criticized on a daily basis, and many of the finger pointers haven't been back in a classroom since they graduated years ago. Furthermore, it is teachers who are directly responsible for successful human beings in all careers and walks of life.

Reader, as you listen to media reports and read the so – called local, state and national report cards on Education, remember the following: Too much "feel good" information will destroy ratings. Our society thirsts for negative news and the media and lobbyists against public education are happy to oblige. Those against public education tower above while we act as carnal beings destroying each other at the core. As a former educator, present Education consultant and ardent supporter of public education, I know firsthand the "War on Miseducation" is actually a war on teachers. Therefore, I choose to write a counter attack of genuine thanks to teachers nationwide, as well as all Education Support Personnel.

Thank you for going into classrooms with children and youth of all different backgrounds filling their hearts and minds with love, learning and leadership. You have to deal with disruptive behavior that has not been addressed at home, and with negative personalities that are a direct result of many of the lemon people who live in these unstable homes. If it weren't for you, many of our future leaders would have no sense of honor, heritage or hope.

Thank you for raising the self – esteem of your students in so many ways. Your smile helps Susan forget that her dad abuses her mom. Your gentle hug helps Brian to forget that both of his parents abandoned him. Your encouragement helps so many others to temporarily forget about the negative comments they receive from and in society. You teach them patriotism, citizenship, teamwork and life – long lessons of learning and responsibility.

Thank you for being a surrogate parent (that's not in the contract). The transportation you provide may cost you your career if you get in an accident and a parent sues you, but if you don't take that risk many students nationwide will have no transportation! The lunch money, supply money, clothes, shoes and hygiene products you provide could cost you your career but you take that risk anyway because you don't want any child to suffer or "be left behind," as President George W. Bush would say.

Thank you for spending your own money out of checks that read: Gross pay/Net pay. The writing is accurate, for teacher's salaries are gross and after taxes, they are caught in the "net' of despair. You are frequently overworked and underpaid. Not only does this disparity in pay with other professionals whose careers are not as scrutinized (because of those served) reflect a lack of respect for teachers, it opens up discussion for a deeper revelation: Does America still have a lack of interest in paying women what they deserve? Although there are men in the profession, teaching is a female dominated field and the television ads beckoning men to join the teaching ranks are increasing daily. Reader, don't believe the hype about vacation time with pay. Teachers are off during the Months of June and July, but many of them have to work to supplement their sub – par incomes; furthermore, they work on part – time jobs during the school year as well. How many doctors, lawyers, engineers, or members of corporate America have part – time jobs? I'm not knocking other career fields, but shouldn't those in the career field which nurtured individuals in all of the above be paid as such? There are those who would have us to be naïve as they exclaim, "Teach for the love and not the money." The "love" by itself does not cover spiritual tithes, monthly bills, food, clothing, or supplies for the students who are loved on a daily basis. How many educators can go in a store and purchase items on "love?" Teachers deserve salaries that mirror their responsibility. Building great minds is no easy task. Increase the pay by placing people above the politics.

Thank you for dealing with the threat of violence every day, and Professional Standards Committees which beckon you to protect yourselves only after the violence has occurred. Students can disrespect you, curse you and physically attack you in America today. Moreover, you have to be "professional" and humble as some parents use profanity laced tirades to keep you in check. You have to listen to some parents who don't realize the version they're getting is coming out of the mouth of a child. You are walking targets for society, but you still press on each day hoping to create a better nation.

Thank you for standing up for God in a system that allows everything but the presence of God. You may not openly encourage your students to pray (you don't want to break the rules), but you don't discourage their thirst for prayer and meditation either. Thank you coaches, teachers and sponsors of extra – curricular activities in school who have the courage to pray. It is God who gave you the ability to educate these young influential minds; don't allow small mis- guided minds to separate you from the love of God. The class – roll is not as vital as God's roll (the book of life) or the role He's given you in the life of the children.

Pray!   Pray!   Pray!

Thank you for embracing colleagues who teach for 10, 15 or 20 years, as well as those who teach 1 year 10, 15 or 20 times. Thank you for being leaders in the midst of administrators who give leadership and support, as well as those who have no professional spines. Thanks for working with parents who genuinely want to see a "School and Community partnership," as well as those who simply want free babysitting for their children everyday. I am well aware that there are pros and cons in every career and life situation, but the pros far outweigh the cons in education. You are now utilizing your reserve nerves teachers, and I sincerely salute you for that!

Thank you for earning more degrees and knowledge in your fields of concentration. Thank you for joining professional organizations such as the National Education Association, Professional Association of Education, American Federation of

Teachers, Phi Delta Kappa and others which promote knowledge, service and commitment to public education. I strongly encourage all educators and education support Personnel to join an organization geared towards protecting the rights of educators. Professionals in all careers utilize organizations of support. Teachers should be no different. Failure to receive support outside of your system may result in a feeling of isolation and despair when issues do arise. Although your site may have a family atmosphere, there is nothing wrong with incorporating extended family. If you have not done so, join an organization ASAP. The camaraderie will make your task less depressing and overwhelming; furthermore, the liabilities and legalities in the profession are ever increasing. Continue to earn more degrees, join more organizations and strengthen the professionalism of your noble career.

Thank you Superintendent's, Principals and Assistant Principals and teachers for promoting community involvement in your schools; allowing those outside education to assist in the molding of our youth is essential. As a motivational speaker, I've been blessed to give messages of hope to thousands of youth as a direct result of cooperative school systems which seek to build the "total human being." The finger pointing lemon people in all careers need to visit the schools more often and uplift the students rather than taunt from the sidelines.

Thank you teachers who seek to build the character of our future leaders. Quite often, educational success is measured by test scores only. One visit to Littleton, Colorado, Jonesboro, Arkansas or other cities and states dissipated by senseless acts of violence will illustrate a dire need for character education. Furthermore, I'm almost certain Osama Bin Laden, Sadam Hussein, Timothy McVeigh and others had high test scores, but their character led to mass destruction and eternal despair. We need to pledge allegiance to those educators who seek to enhance test scores and character. A strong mind can conceive an idea, whether positive or negative. It is an individual's character, however, that puts the idea into action.

Thank you for being marvelous mentors to first year teachers who believe Bloom's Taxonomy, Vtgotsky's Values and Pavlov's principles will be sufficient. The neophytes of the profession receive an abundance of theory in undergraduate programs nationwide, but the children and youth of today prove that practice is far greater than theory. Textbooks are needed sources of valid information, but many of them do not address the culture of contemporary standards. The first year teachers will need your support, supplies and sympathy; thank you for being there for them when the lemon people of the site or system bears down on them with their sour dispositions. Veterans, it is because of you that many new teaches are re – signing contracts in the spring of each year.

Thank you for attending the extra – curricular activities of your students, acting as surrogate parents and cheerleaders. Many of their parents work and cannot attend, but you are there, causing their hearts to swell and giving them greater incentive to do well in the classroom. Your interest in their lives outside of the classroom illustrates to them that you are "human" and not robots with red pens and grade books. Thank you for being chaperons and hosting in – class events on holidays. Believe it or not, there is a direct correlation between your interest in them and their academic performance. Some will succeed in spite of what you do, but so many others will seek to succeed because of your sincerity. Thank you for going the mile past the extra mile.

Thank you teachers for standing tall and bold in the midst of all the symbolic sticks and stones which are meant to break your spirits and symbolic bones. Our public educational system does need work, but so does every facet of the work force in America. In this chapter, however, I offer praise and thanks. You give blood, sweat and tears daily. My fiancé and many of my family members are educators with substance. It takes a genuine spirit, a person with thick skin to survive in this "War." Pat yourselves o the back (with no knives involved). Celebrate and encourage your colleagues and continue to build the Susan's, Brian's, and others. Because of you, great novels are written, lives are saved, advances in technology are made, Supreme Court cases are won, and somewhere in America, a small child looks in the mirror and says, "Because of my teacher, life is worth living."

Reader, at this very moment, I dare you to go and thank a teacher, for he/she is a living epistle of the noblest profession known to mankind.

Thought: I will promote public education as a beacon of uplift in our nation.

"DAP" (Dedicate A Portion)

In memory of the ones who touched my life so that I may in turn touch the lives of others.

You were a light of hope in my <u>life</u> –
Your kinship was so comforting and <u>true</u> –
You gave me serenity in the midst of <u>strife</u> –
I shall <u>Dedicate A Portion </u>of my life to <u>you</u>.

We loved to debate the issues of <u>society</u> –
We used our wits to search for life's <u>clue</u> –
Even when divided, we stood I spiritual <u>unity</u> –
I will <u>Dedicate A Portion</u> of my life to <u>you</u>.

You were of a golden age, and you were <u>blessed</u> –
My years of training will never compare to all you <u>knew</u> –
You gave the family a soothing love, even when <u>stressed</u> –
I must <u>Dedicate A Portion</u> of my life to <u>you</u>.

You were so young by the standards of this <u>earth</u> –
Yet you touched many lives as you <u>grew</u> –
Giving to others always defined your self <u>worth</u> –
I humbly <u>Dedicate A Portion</u> of my life to <u>you</u>.

20
"DAP" (Dedicate A Portion)

It is not our mission to see through each other; it is our mission to see each other through.

In late February 1997, a thunderous knock at my front door frightened me. I cautiously opened the door only to see a look of terror in the eyes of my nephew's father. Before I could scold him for the unnerving knock, he uttered a statement that sent my body into a state of numbness: Preacher, Teddy is in a coma and has a 10% chance to live. It wasn't April, so I knew this was no joke; my life had changed forever. My First cousin, who grew up as my younger brother, was making a swift transition from this world to the next. The last time we spoke, he was preparing to join me in Dublin, Georgia to serve as a panelist on the annual "Black Male Caucus." I called Anthony Irwin and Anthony Jackson to let them know I was headed to Savannah.

Life is so unpredictable! In late October 2001, I received a phone call while traveling in the rush hour traffic of Atlanta, Georgia. Earlier in the day, I'd delivered stimulating speeches at Stone Mountain Middle School. The students really had me in a euphoric state of mind. When I answered the phone, I said a few prophetic words: Well, the dead has finally arisen. Never before had foreshadowing haunted me like it would with Anthony Jackson's response: Greetings my brother, it's funny you should say that. Our brother Anthony Irwin has gone on to be with the Lord. I immediately pulled over and prayed with

Anthony. God drove the rest of the way. During my final conversation with "Mr. I," as he was affectionately called by all of his children at the Winder – Barrow Boys and Girls club, we discussed sports, career moves, my upcoming marriage, health and the nature of women. Anthony succumbed to diabetes, and Teddy lost a life – long battle with Sickle Cell Anemia. I've lost a sister to Cancer (1994) and other relatives and friends to various other entities. I know death well, but I'll never get used to it.

"DAP" is not a chapter about "Despair and Pouting." It's truly geared towards encouraging you to "Dedicate A Portion" of your life to the ones who have passed on into rest. With every project, mission or task, I dedicate a portion of my life to my deceased loved ones. I do not burn candles in their memory because their lights shine in my heart forever.

When Teddy died, I started an active mission of uplift with the Sickle Cell Foundation of Georgia. For the past few years, I've been touched by hundreds of children and youth inflicted with the disease. Every speech, workshop or visit is in his honor. He used to beckon me to rub his aching body, and there were times when I'd get frustrated due to exhaustion. I'd give so much just to be able to rub him once again. Because that is not earthly possible, I must connect with his spirit and be a comfort to those who suffer with the disease. Every experience with "Camp New Hope," "Life Skills Series" and the Sickle Cell Christmas extravaganza enhances my worth in this world. My work with the foundation is extremely vital to my family and me. I look forward to the day when I can set up a scholarship in Teddy's memory. Until then, I'll give my time and talents as I give Teddy and the Sickle Cell Foundation some "DAP."

Reader, don't let the opportunity of "DAP" pass you by. One of the greatest ways of honoring the legacy of our deceased loved ones is living lives of substance and service. Anthony was a genuine friend, business manager and spiritual brother to me.   His heart bled "Boys and Girls Clubs of America;" therefore, I must give more time to the organization. The life of service is indeed the most fulfilling, for our hearts reach the pinnacle of pumping when we give our best to others.

Furthermore, we can give "DAP" by seeking to be great in every endeavor of life we choose, as well as the ones chosen for us through divine guidance.   Anthony's death sparked the completion of <u>CHITLINS.</u> He always beckoned me to finish my book; moreover, when I speak to audiences, especially youth, I use his obituary as a motivational tool. In it are all of his short and long term goals. He wrote them down and somewhere in the universe, he's smiling at me because I have to use his notes to enhance my presentations.

Reader, I am fully aware of the sting and often shock of death. It is very firm, selective and subjective. There is no ambiguity whatsoever. After the news has altered our lives and the funeral is over, we must begin the process of "DAP," fully cognizant of the fact that the Omnipotent hand of God will summon death to merge with us one day. Until then, live life in memory, energy and honor of the ones who touched our lives. Until then, give love and compassion to those who dwell on earth with you. And as you give some "DAP" to the memory of the loved ones, Dedicate Your LIFE TO CHRIST, the one who made it possible for you to give some "DAP."

At this very moment, I dare you to meditate on the memory and then begin to motivate a portion of <u>society</u>.

Thought: "Dedicate A Portion" daily.

21
Poetic Praise

It is not our mission to see through each other; it is our mission to see each other through.

You are welcome! Welcome! Welcome! This chapter is for all the people who have heard or uttered the above statement at some point during their lives. CHITLINS would not be complete without a chapter dedicated to good old fashioned, down home church folks!!! Growing up in the "Black Church," I've laughed until the tears rolled down my face. I've cried as a result of soul – stirring messages of hope. I've shouted hallelujah's, Amen's, and even a few "Help him Lord's." I've attended the Fish Fry's, Baked Sales, bazaar's, and hundreds of other programs. I've heard the following phrases in every denominational cell in the nucleus of the Black church:

- Giving honor to God who is the head of my life.
- You are welcome once, welcome twice, welcome in the name of Jesus Christ.
- Y'all don't hear me (usually uttered by a Pastor whose message is not inspiring the flock)
- The devil is a busy man.
- Take all mistakes for love.
- Charge it to the head, not the heart.
- God is good all the time (and vice versa).

Poetic Praise for the Church History

Note: **The history should be printed in the church program; please allow members and visitors to read it. Don't decrease the energy of the service by reading the entire history.**

Greetings,

> Look around and up and down dear <u>saints</u> –
> God blessed us with the carpet, the pews
> and the <u>paint</u>.

> You remember when the temperature caused many
> To complain and <u>swear</u>?
> Well, He's blessed us with heat and soothed us with
> <u>air</u>.

> He's given us economic prosperity because of
> Tithing and other seeds that were <u>sown</u> -
> And because we have been faithful witnesses –
> Our membership has genuinely <u>grown</u> –

> We've had several pastors down through the
> Years, and they were spiritual <u>stimulators</u> –
> And now we are blessed top have Rev. (name),
> Our chosen <u>emancipator</u>.

> Many have come and many have <u>gone</u> –
> Today, we stand firm in Christ, knowing we must
> hold <u>on</u>.

All around us in this sanctuary, there is <u>progress</u> –
And it evolved from an humble <u>start</u> –
We must remember the sacrifices of our founders –
And keep them in our <u>hearts</u> –
This is God's church and we must all do our <u>part</u>!

For if we are to celebrate another (number) years
Of history – We must work in love and <u>unity</u>
And then we'll move nearer to <u>Calvary</u>!

Do we have any send – by money (the sender wants public credit for the donation, which is usually, less than $5.00).

There are hundreds more, but I just wanted to highlight a few. All people, regardless of race, are welcome at the "Black Church" in America. I've been to all types, and there is a form of healing in each; if you find one that does not move you to action, move on. Also, if you visit one that uses only the traditional same old greetings, welcomes and salutations, pass on the following poetic praises of creative uplift. These poetic praises were not written to replace the traditional ones, but it does help to have Omnipotent inspired options.

<u>Poetic Praise for Visitors</u>

Exclaimer: Greetings,
Will our special guests please <u>stand</u> –
Now Brothers and Sisters of (Church name), let's
Give them a Holy <u>hand</u>. (pause to applaud).

We are truly blessed by your presence on <u>today</u> –
For God is the potter and we are His <u>clay</u> –

Relax, rejoice and enjoy the <u>Service</u> –
Your praises to Him make Satan <u>nervous</u>.

And as you sit in this place of Spiritual
<u>Unity</u> –

Know that you came as a visitor, but you'll
Leave as <u>family</u>!

Poetic Praise for an Anniversary

Exclaimer: Greetings to the descendants of those Spiritual
Soldiers whose shoulder we stand upon!
We've faced trials and tribulations down
through the <u>years</u> –
We've lost many loved ones and cried many
<u>tears</u>!

But through it all, it has been God's grace and
<u>mercy</u> –
And now we exclaim, "Hallelujah" for another
<u>Anniversary</u>.
Our forefathers and mothers laid the <u>foundation</u> –

And we have witnessed many spiritual

sensations–
God has anointed us in <u>unity</u> – so
we must forget the negative "<u>used to be</u>,"
for if we are to move closer to <u>Calvary</u> –
we must live in oneness on this and every
<u>Anniversary</u>!

Poetic Praise for Funerals

Once again we come to this sacred <u>place</u> –
Death hands us a cup we'd rather not <u>taste</u> –

Once again we gather at this sacred <u>place</u> –
Jesus gently sips the tears from each loved ones
<u>face</u>–
Once again we celebrate and mourn in this
sacred <u>place</u> –

Our living relative does thirst; the drink of
bitterness we must <u>erase</u> –

Once again, a family reunion in this sacred
<u>place</u> – we should get drunk in the spirit and
a loving <u>embrace</u>.

Once again, we assemble in this sacred <u>place</u> –
Another opportunity to grow closer to Jesus or
Send our souls to <u>waste</u>.

Poetic Praise for "Family and Friends" day

Greetings –

    We are gathered here today in Spiritual <u>unity</u> –
    To uplift the name of Christ with our dear
    friends and <u>family</u>.

    Whether your journey took a day, a few minutes
    Or an <u>hour</u> –
    We will praise His name and give thanks for
    His <u>power</u>.

    Hand in hand and heart and heart, under
    The blood we are all <u>kin</u>, and when we
    Spread the gospel instead of the gossip, we
    Reduce this worldly <u>sin</u>!

    So answer my brothers and my Sisters when
    Family and family are <u>called</u> – And remember
    We are free, because Jesus paid it <u>all</u>!

Poetic Praise for Choir Programs

Greetings –

On today, we come with praise –
Our voices in song we joyfully raise –

Sopranos, Alto's, Tenor's and Bass –
We sing hallelujah with a smile on each face.

The director is directing and the Musicians
Are playing –
The spirit is high and Satan won't be staying.

Guest Choirs have joined us from all over
town –

Marching in the choir stand with melodious
Sounds.

The Congregation will be clapping hands on today
And there will be a rumbling of the feet –
Voices are raised, full of praise, then our
Program will be complete.

Poetic Praise for the Usher's Ministry

Greetings,

We are the first faces you <u>see</u> –
As you enter God's <u>sanctuary</u>.

We give you a program and even a <u>fan</u> –
We beckon you to sit and we urge you to <u>stand</u>.

We are here as the doorkeepers and a
Form of <u>protection</u> –
We are the ones who receive your gifts to
God during <u>collection</u>.

We even discipline the children, and keep order
Until service is <u>through</u> –
We are a marvelous ministry draped in black,
White or blue.

So as we celebrate our place in God's
Vineyard, we are truly proud to <u>be</u> –
The doorkeepers of love ordained from above in
God's <u>sanctuary</u>!

Poetic Praise for Revival

Greetings,

Exclaimer: In this world of broken hearts, one
                        more
                        Day we have <u>survived</u> –

                        So we came tonight with Praises in
                        our Mouths, it's time to get <u>revived</u>!

Congregation: A <u>Revival</u> for Our <u>Survival</u>!

Exclaimer: With prayers and praises and
                        soothing <u>songs</u> –
                        We'll remain steadfast through the
                        storm, revived And <u>strong</u>!

Congregation: A <u>Revival</u> for Our <u>Survival</u>!

Exclaimer: Sickness and Violence throughout the
                        <u>Nation</u> – but the Word shall come
                        forth as <u>Confirmation</u>! We are so
                        blessed just to be <u>Alive</u>, stand up for
                        Jesus and let's be <u>Revived</u>!

Congregation: A <u>Revival</u> for Our <u>Survival</u>!

(Repeat until there is a thunderous congregational praise!!!!!)

Reader, go back to your church and take these poetic praises with you; sit down with the other members and create more. The services must be upbeat and fresh. There is nothing like a fresh new word coming forth. Summon the creative ones and form a "Poetic Praise" ministry. I excluded prayers because I sincerely believe prayers are meant to come only from the individual uttering them. If you sincerely disagree with "Poetic Praise," just say, "Help him Lord." But if you are moved to action and utter thanks, I boldly say, "You are welcome, welcome, welcome!

22
Clearance Sale

It is not our mission to see through each other; it is our mission to see each other through.

This chapter is dedicated to consumers and employees who are fed up with the lemon people they encounter on a daily basis. When I do staff development workshops, the number one complaint of the staff members is dealing with rude, obnoxious customers. I fully understand their complaint because I've been face to face with a lemon disposition who society called "consumer." The only thing he/she consumed, however, was the positive nature of the environment. Employees do not deserve to be badgered by negative customers, and employers must work vigorously to protect the well – being of the individuals they employ. If you are employed in any career where you are not genuinely valued, you may need to update your resume. If profits are the only bottom line, you may want to place yourself on clearance and move on to a situation where you are a person and not a puppet. I boldly salute those individuals who do their best and sincerely believe in customer satisfaction. I frown upon consumers who badger staff members for no apparent reason.

We all know that there are two sides to every story. The initial paragraph dealt with heads; now I must focus on the tail, the ones we as informative consumers are beckoned to kiss on a daily basis. In the past year, I've changed cellular phone companies, cleaners, department stores and restaurants due to the lemon people who were employed by these businesses. As a consumer (not a lemon consumer), you have the right to fast, efficient courteous service because you are spending your money! How many times have you spent money in an establishment, only to leave frustrated because of the negative attitude of an employee? When consumers badger employees, they can turn to their employers for support. They don't deserve to be treated negatively, and my advice to anyone caught in a confrontation with a customer is to walk away and get your manager! Now reader, what about the cooperative consumer who has no one to turn to? Consumers, if you are fed up with the service, here are a few scenarios and options to consider:

(1). You go into your favorite restaurant and receive the waiter/waitress from hell. He/she is rude and negative. You are being patient because everyone has a bad day, but the food is just as mediocre as your server. Remember, this is your favorite restaurant; furthermore, it's getting late and you fear long – lines or "closed" signs at other restaurants. What should you do?

(A). Endure the negative and chalk it up to happenstance.

(B). Get rude with the waiter/waitress and then eat.

(C). Get rude with the waiter/waitress and leave.

(D). Ask for the manager and politely explain the situation.

(E). Ask for the manager and let your emotions lead you.

The only win –win situation here is (D). The manager is more likely to hear and listen to your complaint/concern and act upon it. Furthermore, when the manager says that customary line, "What can I do to make your evening better?" respond by requesting a complimentary meal on a different night with a different waiter/waitress. Don't use the waiter/waitress as a personal target. Emphasize the dissatisfaction with the environment, not the person. If you choose (B) or (E), you may end up being escorted out by the local authorities or being asked to leave the premises. If you choose (C), you'll only take that anger and frustration out on others, namely those spending the evening with you. If you choose (A), you are forfeiting your rights as a consumer and advocating the negative behavior of the server. (D) is not the only option, but it is a win – win situation.

(2).   You take an item back that has the store seal on it. You cannot get a refund because you don't have a receipt; however, your request of exchanging the item is also denied. What should you do?

(A).   Get loud and rude with the store employee.

(B).   Politely ask for a manager.

(C).   Get rude and take the same item home.

(D).   Throw the item on the counter and walk away in disgust.

The only win – win situation is (B). If someone is not in an authoritative position but makes authoritative decisions, always question that; do so, however, with tact and discretion. In other words, don't accept a "no" from someone who is not in a position to tell you "yes." Option (A) will get you escorted from the store. With options (C) and (D), you lose time, value of merchandise and money. No matter how difficult, if you want to win and receive customer satisfaction, always be lemonade in the midst of the lemon people.

Reader, here are a few other tips to aid you as consumers:

(A).   Ask for all policies in writing. Legitimate businesses have policies in writing just as schools and organizations have mission statements.

(B).   Do not accept mediocre service.

(C).   Be loyal "only" to those businesses that treat people as humans and not robots.

(D).   Create a positive environment by first illustrating a positive attitude.

(E).   If it's a franchise, get the store number, manager's name, negative employee's name, etc.

(F).   If there are several stores with one owner, make sure all stores policies are consistent.

(G).   Put yourself in the other person's shoes.

(H).   Keep all receipts and records if possible.

(I).   Don't shop with lemon people.

Reader, it doesn't matter which side of the coin you are on; we all need to use our heads and stop using our tails as a means of communicating and/or dealing with one another. We all have bad days when we are lemon people in some form or fashion, but we must not allow our sour dispositions to usurp the positive energy of others. If you are a consumer, be kind, fair and respectful, even in the midst of confusion. You will face a win – win situation 90% of the time.

If you are an employer/employee, have the same traits and beyond. The difference between you and the consumer is real: The consumer pays your salary!! If you lose consumers, you will ultimately lose your hours, salary and your position. Furthermore, consumers will spread either the gospel (positive aspect) or gossip (negative aspects) when it comes to your business. The rude behavior must be put on clearance, marked down to 0% and out of style forever. At this moment, I dare you to have a "All negative items must got to make room for the positive" mentality.

Thought: As a consumer, I will consume the positive and spread it. As an employer/employee, I will make my workplace an environment of sincere service and angelic attitudes.

"America Will Rise Again"

It is not our mission to see through <u>each other</u> –
It is our mission to see each other <u>through</u> –
Terrorists sought to cripple the fiber of <u>America</u> –
But no evil force will paralyze the spirit of the Red, White and <u>Blue</u> –
In spite of these senseless acts of terror and <u>Sin</u> –
America the beautiful will rise <u>again</u>!

They attacked Somerset, the Pentagon, and the Twin <u>Towers</u> –
It was a solemn day and a shocking <u>hour</u> –
They attempted to demolish the core of our nation's <u>power</u> –
But in this garden called "the World," America is God's most precious <u>flower</u> –
Cells of terror shall not <u>win</u> –
The nucleus of America will rise <u>again</u>!

Our President stood tall, firm and <u>great</u> –
With national prayer and a promise to <u>retaliate</u> –
Members of Congress stood BI – partisan to <u>illustrate</u> –
Regardless of your party, race, religion or <u>creed</u> –
It is a universal healing we all do <u>need</u>!

United we stick, divided we're <u>stuck</u> –
We need God's blessing not good <u>luck</u>!
For when it appears that our nation's strength is growing
<u>thin</u> –
Know in your hearts, America will rise <u>again</u>.

So let healing begin <u>nationwide</u> –
Let Faith, Hope, Charity, and Love <u>abide</u> –
Our children and youth can recite the <u>preamble</u> –
But we must set the sincere <u>example</u> –
The enemy has come with an evil <u>grin</u> –
But the laughter of America will rise <u>again</u>!

23

Reflect, Protect, Connect Each Other...

It is not our mission to see through each other; it is our mission to see each other through.

Certainly the recent catastrophic events have caused all Americans to re - think, re – focus, and re – assess every aspect of their lives. It seems as if tragedy has birthed an ironic sense of triumph; on nearly every billboard, Marquee, or sign in America, we see the following spiritual request: God Bless America. Yes, that is our noble sincere universal national prayer request. There is one, however, even more vital at this time, a request I heard uttered from the mouth of my Uncle Charles, a spiritual warrior: It's now time for America to bless God. The Creator has never stopped blessing us, even in the midst of the September 11th mess! Out of the mess came a profound message: we must endeavor to reflect, protect and connect each other.

Reflect

Regardless of your spiritual preference, you realize we are all made in the image of an Omnipotent, Omniscient, Omnipresent God. Therefore, there is greatness in all of us. When we acknowledge this, we are reflecting Him, thus reflecting each other because He is in all of us. We do have choices, however. We can manifest compassion, kindness, respect and strength as we live on a daily basis, or smear the reflection with hatred, jealousy, laziness, and low self – esteem and disrespect. When we reflect each other in His name, race, creed, culture and other differences are celebrated not degraded. When we sincerely reflect each other, we are more capable of harvesting the talents that lie within each of us. Go look in the mirror reader. The reflection you see is actually the God in you, the same God who created the thousands who look like you and the millions who don't.

Protect

When we think of protection, uniformed officers, security systems and weapons usually come to mind. All are valid in some way, shape or form, but the protection I'm most concerned about can only be effective through the power of human healing. The same God who gave us the ability to reflect each other, is the same one who has planted the seed of protection in all of us. Protecting each other is not always easy, for there are the lemon people of society who beckon us to physically, verbally, and emotionally badger each other. We must be stronger than the lemon people, and in the midst of their mission to destroy, we must work steadfast to build. We must protect each other with positive communication, genuine unity, (not ornamental unity born out of tragedy only), and benevolence. We must work together to eradicate racism, violence, substance selling and using, miseducation, poverty and many other ills that taint our great nation. Our youth must see sincere examples of protection if they are expected to be the protectors and leaders in the New Millennium. No longer can we be re – active passive beings when it comes to protection.

We must be strong, pro – active citizens prepared to stand up for the rights of those who we share this soil with.

Connect

When objects are connected, they became more powerful; the same is true for people. As Americans, we must use our unique, beautiful, bountiful backgrounds to connect the human spirit we all share. In the span of an hour, terrorists took all of our division and sadistically launched it in our souls, eating the core of our way of life. Now we stand as Americans, still faced with many of the issues that reflected our lives before September 11, 2001. In order to connect each other, we must address those issues, many of which stem from a false sense of superiority over each other. In order to connect each other, we must practice honor and humility. We all shed blood, sweat and tears, and we all want to live prosperous, productive lives, in some way, shape or form. Every individual must examine him/herself. Every family, community, town, city and state must examine itself. The connection that we have witnessed during the months after the horrific attacks must not be a symbol of temporary medicine. It must be a permanent national cure that beckons human beings to step forth and fight injustice wherever it may arise. The task of keeping national unity alive will not be an easy one, but if the people who choose to be lemonade (positive, progressive, pro – active) heavily outnumber and outweigh the lemon people (negative, regressive, re – active), the task will be less daunting. As the American Flags wave in the wind with patriotic pride atop stadiums, arenas, buildings and homes nationwide, let us wave to each other as we go forward from place to place seeking the greatest prizes of them all: peace of mind and happiness.

At this very moment, I dare you to pledge allegiance to uplift your fellow human being.

Thought: I will seek to reflect, protect and connect on a daily basis.

ABOUT THE AUTHOR

Keith "Preacher" Brown (The Motivator of the Millennium) was born in Savannah, Georgia and raised in Jamaica, New York. After being labeled "Special – Ed," "At – Risk," and potential "Menace to Society," Keith dedicated his life to overcoming those stigmatization's and graduated with honors from Savannah State University with a degree in Communications/English. He did his graduate work in English at Georgia Southern University and earned certification in education. Keith is a former high school English, Speech and Drama educator, and a Technical College Adjunct faculty member. In 1999, he "stepped out on faith" to become a full time Motivational Speaker. His "faith" journey has led him to "Showtime at the Apollo" (spoken – word) and many Colleges, Universities, schools, churches and foundations as a speaker and workshop facilitator. He is an Educational Consultant, Legislative Liaison, a member of the National Speakers Association, and the American Federation of Radio and Television Artists. He has been inducted in Phi Delta Kappa, Professional Fraternity in Education, Who's Who Among America's Teachers, and is a member of the Outstanding Young Men of America.

"Preacher" currently resides in both Atlanta and Savannah, Georgia.

To order additional books or to schedule a seminar for your school, organization, convention, or exposition, log on to:

www.keithlbrown.com

Or write to us at:

Regal Publishing
2 Burbank Blvd
Savannah, Georgia 31419

Or

Keith L. Brown Publications
1524 Arcadian Street
Savannah, Georgia 31405
e-mail: **preacher133@yahoo.com**

KEITH L. BROWN
MOTIVATOR OF THE MILLENNIUM

ORDER FORM
KEITH L. BROWN
PUBLICATIONS

BOOKS

CHITLINS is a manual for spiritual, economic, cultural, social and intellectual growth. Its chapters deal with "real life" issues and provide realistic solutions. The book challenges traditions that keep people in the web of ignorance, and it commends individuals who desire to uplift others in thought, word and action. It is a genuine literary healing instrument designed for a nation crying out for hope. CHITLINS is an excellent book for anyone seeking to reach the pinnacle of progress and happiness.
By Keith L. Brown - Cost: $25.00

OTHER PUBLICATIONS

Loose the Lemons is a booklet designed to make individuals aware of the negative people who influence the lives of others. Accordingly, negative people are referred to as "Lemon People". This is an excellent supplement for classroom "character education" activities. A Teacher's Guide and Student Journal Guide are also available.

By Keith L. Brown - Cost:$10   Student Journal $5   Teacher's Guide $20

Super-vision not Supervision is a booklet that demonstrates the importance of creating a super-vision that directs your life instead of having your life directed by the supervision of others. This booklet is about taking risks and focusing on your future. This is an excellent supplement for classroom "character education" activities. A Teacher's Guide and Student Journal Guide are also available.

By Keith L. Brown - Cost:$10   Student Journal $5   Teacher's Guide $20

Tongue Twister is a booklet that emphasizes the difference between Formal Language or "Standard American English" and Informal Language or "Slang". This booklet illustrates the significance of knowing and using formal language. This is an excellent tool for teachers and is guaranteed to enhance classroom communication skills. A Teacher's Guide and Student Journal Guide are also available.

By Keith L. Brown - Cost:$10   Student Journal $5   Teacher's Guide $20

Voices vs. Choices is a booklet that highlights the importance of making the right choice. An emphasis is placed on building self-trust and relying upon your inner voice instead of the voices of others. This is an excellent supplement for classroom "character education" activities. A Teacher's Guide and Student Journal Guide are also available.

By Keith L. Brown - Cost:$10   Student Journal $5   Teacher's Guide $20

SEE REVERSE SIDE FOR ORDERING INFORMATION

Order Form

Publication Name	Unit Price	Number of Copies	Total Price

_____ Check Enclosed

_____ Money Order Enclosed

_____ Purchase Order Enclosed
         P.O.#_____

Subtotal _____

Total Price_____

Shipping_____

Total Amt. Due_____

Please ship my order to:
(**We cannot ship to P.O. boxes!**)

Name _____

Title _____

Organization_____

Street Address_____

City_____State_____Zip_____

Phone Number _____

Email _____

Standard Shipping	
Up to $15	$4
$15.01 to $20	$6
$20.01 to $40	$8
$40.01 to $60	$10
$60.01 to $80	$12
$80.01 to $100	$14
$100.01 to $150	$16.50
$150.01 to $200	$19
$200.01 and up	$19 plus $2.50 for each added $50 of order

Mail Order To: Publications Department
Keith Brown Publications, 1524 Arcadian Street, Savannah, Georgia 31405
1-800-725-2694 pin#0726 or 678-770-2553

Order Form

Publication Name	Unit Price	Number of Copies	Total Price

_____ Check Enclosed

_____ Money Order Enclosed

_____ Purchase Order Enclosed
P.O.#_____

Subtotal _____

Total Price_____

Shipping_____

Total Amt. Due_____

Please ship my order to:
(**We cannot ship to P.O. boxes!**)

Name _____

Title _____

Organization_____

Street Address_____

City_____State_____Zip_____

Phone Number _____

Email _____

Standard Shipping	
Up to $15	$4
$15.01 to $20	$6
$20.01 to $40	$8
$40.01 to $60	$10
$60.01 to $80	$12
$80.01 to $100	$14
$100.01 to $150	$16.50
$150.01 to $200	$19
$200.01 and up	$19 plus $2.50 for each added $50 of order

Mail Order To: Publications Department
Keith Brown Publications, 1524 Arcadian Street, Savannah, Georgia 31405
1-800-725-2694 pin#0726 or 678-770-2553